PENGUIN BOOKS
INDIA

Dr Bimal Jalan is a former governor of the Reserve Bank of India. He has held several positions in the government, including those of finance secretary and chairman of the Economic Advisory Council to the prime minister. He was a nominated member of the Rajya Sabha from 2003 to 2009 and was chairman of the Expenditure Management Commission from 2014 to 2016. He has also represented India on the boards of the IMF and the World Bank.

Dr Jalan has been associated with a number of academic and public institutions, including the Indian Statistical Institute, Kolkata; the Institute of Economic Growth, New Delhi; the Centre for Development Studies, Thiruvananthapuram (as chairman); and the National Council of Applied Economic Research, New Delhi.

INDIA

PRIORITIES *for the* FUTURE

BIMAL JALAN

PENGUIN BOOKS

An imprint of Penguin Random House

PENGUIN BOOKS

USA | Canada | UK | Ireland | Australia
New Zealand | India | South Africa | China | Singapore

Penguin Books is part of the Penguin Random House group of companies
whose addresses can be found at global.penguinrandomhouse.com

Published by Penguin Random House India Pvt. Ltd
4th Floor, Capital Tower 1, MG Road,
Gurugram 122 002, Haryana, India

First published in Viking by Penguin Random House India 2017
Chapter 1 reproduced with permission of
Oxford University Press © Oxford University Press 1992
Published in Penguin Books 2018

Copyright © Bimal Jalan 2017

ISBN 9780143444565

Typeset in Adobe Garamond Pro by Manipal Digital Systems, Manipal
Printed at Repro India Limited

Contents

Preface

Until 2014, in India, when the present government took office with a majority of members in Parliament, there were as many as twelve different governments in the thirty-four years since 1980. Of these, four multiparty coalitions survived their five-year terms with occasional setbacks and shifts in the composition of parties supporting them from the inside or outside. Excluding these four coalition governments that completed their full term, the average term of office of the remaining eight governments was less than two years.

Naturally, considering the government's short life expectancy in office and multiparty coalitions, and each party with different political agendas, it was not feasible for any government to initiate political reforms of a type that could reduce the discretionary powers of ministers or otherwise reduce the role of the Central government in the allocation of financial resources across different states.

Since 2014, the typical political profile of the government, with a single majority party in Parliament, has changed dramatically. Now, it is entirely feasible for the government to launch political reforms to reduce the discretionary powers of independent ministers belonging to different parties and to make political changes that can effectively reduce corruption and administrative bottlenecks in the delivery of services. This book is an attempt to identify some priorities for the future that can be implemented within a relatively short period of two to three years, until 2019, when the present government will complete its first term.

In some ways, 1980 was a watershed year in the nation's post-Independence political history, as, previously, governments were formed mainly by the Congress party, which enjoyed a majority in Parliament for as long as thirty years after Independence, followed by two short-term governments during 1977–79. The first section in the book, 'India: Then', highlights certain developments mainly in India's economic policies during the period 1980–2000. During this time, the government formed by the Congress in 1980, with Rajiv Gandhi as prime minister, initiated a process of loosening the direct controls and regulatory framework for investments by the private sector as well as enabling the freer movement of foreign direct investment (FDI) into the country. However, during this period, there was no major change in the role of the government or the public sector in the economy. In the 1980s, India also suffered a persistent balance-of-payment problem, with very low foreign-exchange reserves. As a result, India's capacity to meet its import requirements had also become extremely insufficient. In order to tackle these problems, there was an urgent need for a new development strategy and financial reforms to generate higher growth.

The second section, 'India: Now (2000–15)', deals with the economic and political situation persisting since the beginning of the twenty-first century and highlights some important priorities for the future that can help India realize its full potential as one of the fastest-growing emerging economies in the world. This section also deals with certain issues relating to the separation of powers among the three organs of the state: the legislature, the judiciary and the executive. This may be of particular interest to those who are interested in ensuring that the tussle between or encroachment by either the legislature or the executive in the domain of the judiciary is avoided, irrespective of which party or coalitions of parties is in power.

I am grateful to Satish Choudhary for his meticulous work in preparing the manuscript for publication, and to K.D. Sharma for his help in putting together the vast material, stretching over several decades. I am also very grateful to Udayan Mitra, Ranjana Sengupta and Meru Gokhale of Penguin Random House for their advice, guidance and painstaking efforts to improve the contents of the book. I also appreciate greatly the work done by Rachita Raj for copy-editing the book at very short notice. Without their encouragement and support, this book could not have been completed.

Introduction

In 2017—the year of this book's publication—India will celebrate the seventieth year of its independence. On 15 August 1947, when India became independent, in a celebrated and oft-quoted passage in his address to the nation, Jawaharlal Nehru said, 'Long years ago, we made a tryst with destiny, and now the time comes when we shall redeem our pledge, not wholly or in full measure, but very substantially. At the stroke of the midnight hour, when the world sleeps, India will awake to life and freedom.'

As we look back to that day, there is certainly much to rejoice in what our nation has been able to achieve. Seventy years ago, in the light of India's poverty and diversity, there were not too many political observers who believed that Indian democracy would survive for long. Over time, however, India's democratic system has not only survived but is universally regarded as a role model for the peaceful transfer of power from one government to another after periodic elections.

The Indian economy, which for quite some time—in the 1960s and the 1970s—was in the doldrums, also recovered and has shown steady growth since the beginning of the 1980s. The economy's potential for even faster growth is now believed to be high, according to experts from all over the world. The view that India will become one of the dominant economies of the world by the middle of the twenty-first century is fast gaining traction.

At the same time, it is important to recognize that while all this is true, the working of our political and economic system requires constant vigilance and the launching of reforms, as necessary, from time to time. The processes of governance, the distribution of power among the different agencies of the state, the functioning of political parties and the work of Parliament must be under periodic review. The real issue now is not whether India's democratic electoral system has proved its sustainability, but whether it can be made to work better in the light of political developments over time.

In terms of governance structure, the twenty-year period of 1980–2000 was significantly different from the first fifteen years, i.e., from 2000–15, of the twenty-first century. During the earlier period, there were as many as nine different governments in power at the Centre at various points in time, including two Congress governments, led by Indira Gandhi and Rajiv Gandhi, which were in office for their full terms. During the 1990s, however, there were seven different governments formed by the coalition of parties in Parliament, of which as many as six governments were in office for less than one year.

In contrast, during 2000–14, there were three governments that completed their full terms, one led by the National Democratic Alliance (NDA), followed by two Congress-led coalitions. Currently, since 2014, for the first time in the twenty-first century, we have a new government formed by a party that commands a majority on its own. In terms of governance and politics, the situation is now dramatically different. The present government is now in a position to launch the major reforms or administrative changes that may be required to realize India's full economic potential of high growth combined with a faster rate of poverty alleviation.

As is clear from the table of contents at the beginning, the book is divided into two sections, 'India Then (1980–2000)' and 'India Now (2000–15)'. The first section highlights the initiation of the reform process during the twenty-year period of 1980–2000, when there were several different governments in power. The second section highlights the economic situation at the beginning of the twenty-first century and the changes that occurred in governance and the administrative system under the previous three governments that were in power for their full terms. The last chapter in this section highlights some important priorities for the future in the areas of politics and governance in the light of recent developments in the economy.

On 18 January 1991, India's foreign-exchange reserves stood at only $930 million. This was barely sufficient to meet even the daily cash requirements of an economy of India's size. But for a loan from the International Monetary Fund (IMF), which was approved in mid-January of 1991, there was a strong possibility that India would have been forced to default on its international obligations for the first time in its post-Independence history.

In the light of India's highly disappointing record of the way in which the economy was organized during the years before 1990, the first essay in this book outlines a ten-point programme of action which, in future, could lay the foundations of sustainable growth and could also be implemented quickly.

As it happens, the suggestions made in the essay, published twenty-five years ago in 1991, are still relevant. Some of the suggestions of contemporary importance, for example, are:

- Early action to eliminate revenue deficit altogether;
- Reorganization of public-sector enterprises, particularly loss-making ones, through disinvestment;
- Replacement of direct physical controls by non-discretionary fiscal, credit and financial regulations;
- Decentralization of planning and financing of public projects to state governments;
- Ensuring that the highest priority is assigned to achieving full literacy within a decade;
- Reducing administrative costs in the delivery of services to the poor; and
- Making the administrative system at the Centre and the states more functional and accountable to the people.

The second chapter, 'Controls, Regulations and the State', written in 1996, highlights the slow progress in reducing the role of the state in controlling and regulating the allocation of resources in the economy, or for that matter, in improving the functioning of the administrative system for the benefit of the people. As it happened, over time, there was, in fact, a vast expansion of the Central government, which, by early 1990, had as many as 3.5 million employees (in comparison to the total employment figures of about 4.5 million persons in manufacturing in the private organized sector). The number of ministries and departments at the Centre and in the states also proliferated.

In the context of the above background of developments during the 1980s, Chapter 3, in the section 'India Then', highlights certain priorities for initiating a new strategy that would ensure economic stability, reduce high fiscal deficits and accelerate public investment in infrastructure as well as loss-making public-sector enterprises. A basic point made in this chapter is that the key to accelerating growth in India, as elsewhere, lies in higher investment in industry. This was particularly so at low points in industrial and business cycles when the current output was growing slowly. In looking for a strategy for higher industrial growth in the 1990s, this chapter tries to identify those factors that could facilitate higher investment by industry in new plants and technologies, and significantly accelerate India's industrial and overall growth rate.

The fourth chapter in this section deals with the evolving role of finance and development. This role has, of course, always been recognized. However, the events of the last few years, particularly after the East Asian crisis of 1997, have brought to the fore the critical role of the financial system in determining the stability and sustainability of the real economy. As a result, the reform of the financial system, and the rules and codes that should govern the conduct of financial business, figure high on the domestic agenda for reform as well as on the international agenda for global cooperation.

The most important lesson emerging from the Asian crisis is the need to be vigilant about developments—domestic and international—that may impinge on a country's financial relations with the rest of the world. The process of integration of worldwide financial markets has resulted in product innovation and greater efficiency, but it has also made developing countries subject to greater vulnerability and new risks. Strong fundamentals alone cannot provide full immunity from a crisis. There is a need to take early preventive action, to build firewalls and to keep some safety nets handy.

In the light of the above discussion, the fourth chapter ends with a review of the recent Indian experience in financial management and lays down some priorities for the future. In working out these priorities, it is important to remember that financial reforms and liberalization of markets are the means to an end—not ends in themselves.

The second section in the book, 'India Now (2000–15)', deals with India's economic and political situation since the beginning of the twenty-first century and highlights some important priorities for the future for the country to realize its full potential as one of the fastest-growing emerging economies. The first essay in this section (in Chapter 5) emphasizes the need for India to move towards more and deeper economic reforms in the future.

In addition to economic reforms, which figure prominently in the national discourse, it is now essential to embark on an urgent programme to revitalize the governance and public delivery systems at all levels of the government—the Centre, state and districts. Without strengthening the ability of the government to do what it alone can do, and narrowing the focus of its activities to what matters most for the future development of the country—education, health, clean environment and a functioning infrastructure—India cannot adequately seize the opportunities that lie ahead.

Chapter 6, titled 'Politics and Governance', deals with some issues that require action at the highest level of the government to improve governance and delivery of public service to the people. Chapter 7, 'Separation of Powers: The Myth and the Reality', deals with issues relating to the separation of powers among the three organs of the state—the legislature, the judiciary and the executive.

The last chapter of the book deals with certain important 'Priorities for the Future', particularly with respect to the reform of politics and governance so that India is able to realize its full economic potential as an emerging power. The objective is to put these priorities together in a form that makes it feasible to implement them within a relatively short period of time—hopefully, before the next General Election in 2019.

INDIA THEN (1980–2000)

1

Development Strategy and Performance[*]

The year 1990 was among the cruellest in India's post-Independence economic history. A new government took over in December 1989, at a time when the fiscal deficit was high and the foreign-exchange reserves low (covering only about six weeks of imports). The Budget, introduced in March 1990, made an attempt to reduce the fiscal deficit and begin the process of correction in the balance-of-payments position. For a while the economic situation seemed to show some improvement. The fiscal deficit was, by the end of August 1990, significantly lower than in the previous year, and foreign-exchange reserves were slightly higher (in contrast to a sharp decline in the reserves in the corresponding period of the previous year). However, there was a dramatic reversal of this situation in the next few months. Consequent upon the annexation

---

* Edited version of Chapter 1 in *India's Economic Crisis: The Way Ahead* (Oxford: University Press, 1991).

of Kuwait by Iraq on 2 August 1990, crude oil prices rose sharply. Within a period of six weeks, these prices doubled. Even though the Gulf War did not last long, India's fragile economy was badly shaken.

The direct economic impact of the conflict in the Gulf was exacerbated by domestic social and political developments. The implementation of the Mandal Commission report was announced by the government on 7 August 1990. This led to massive student protests and a breakdown of the law-and-order situation in several parts of the country. This event was followed by conflict in Ayodhya over the Ram Janambhoomi–Babri Masjid issue. For four weeks or so, there was further disruption, conflict and high tension. A direct political consequence of the same was the fall of the government on 7 November 1990. Another minority government took office in mid-November. This series of events, in tandem with the conflict in the Gulf, was enough to shake international confidence in India's economic viability. The country found it more and more difficult to borrow internationally, and there was also an adverse impact on the inflow of funds from non-resident Indians. During the 1980s it had seemed, for a while, that the economy was poised for a breakthrough. The Economic Survey of the Government of India for 1988–89, in fact, announced that 'the Indian economy is now on a new growth path'. The growth rate for the decade was certainly higher, and there was evidence of substantial growth in output in several sophisticated industries, such as electronics. The capital markets were buoyant, and industrial growth averaged more than 8 per cent for the period 1985–90. During this period there was also some reassessment of the control system. A number of committees were appointed, which submitted reports on trade policy, public-sector policy and on the matter of a potential shift from physical to financial control. Each of these committees recommended a move away from quantitative control to fiscal methods of economic management. Several recommendations made by these committees were implemented, and there was considerable loosening of direct controls, particularly in the field of industrial licensing.

The gains from the policy changes of the 1980s, however, proved to be temporary. The growth in industrial production was overshadowed by a balance-of-payments crisis of unprecedented magnitude. There was a large accumulation of external debt and a widening of the current-account deficit, which rendered the economy highly vulnerable to external and internal shocks. Between September and November 1990, foreign-exchange reserves, which were already low, fell by nearly 50 per cent. The effort to reduce the rate of fall in foreign-exchange reserves meant a severe curtailment in the imports of both oil and industrial raw materials and components. The domestic prices of petroleum products were increased sharply to compensate for the rise in international prices. Although unavoidable, this added to costs and prices in the economy. By the end of 1990, the economic situation became highly precarious. Exchange reserves were at rock bottom, inflation had crossed the double-digit level and was moving higher, and the fiscal deficit was sharply widening. Paradoxically, this severe financial crisis was taking place at a time when the real sectors of the economy seemed to be performing reasonably well. As a result of an excellent monsoon, agricultural production was at its peak; industrial production was increasing at the rate of over 8 per cent per annum and exports were doing well. The financial crisis was, however, of such magnitude that gains in the real sector were severely eroded by a crisis of confidence and the shortage of international liquidity.

This was the dismal economic situation at the beginning of 1991. India had been affected by external shocks before, but the short-term situation had never been as difficult. The only previous parallel was perhaps the situation in 1958—with one difference. Then, the world environment was favourable for development. The first Aid India Consortium was organized in 1959. Both multilateral institutions and bilateral donors came forward with massive external assistance to finance the Second Five-Year Plan. The situation was very different in 1991, and there was no equivalent response from the international community.

Underlying this sense of despondence, there was a widespread feeling in the country that something was missing or wrong in the way we had organized our economy over the previous four decades. The economy moved from one crisis to another, poverty was still massive and the quality of public and social services had deteriorated.

A basic premise of India's Five-Year Plans, as well as the early development literature, was that the required administrative response would be forthcoming in abundant measure in order to meet the tasks assigned to the different levels of administration—from the Centre to the village level. The administration was expected to work in complete harmony and coordination in order to carry out these various tasks. It must be said to the credit of our early planners that they explicitly recognized the vast administrative requirements of the strategy they visualized. Thus, the Second Five-Year Plan devoted a whole chapter to spelling out 'Administrative Tasks and Organization'. It clearly stated that 'while the area of agreement on matters of policy is considerable, doubt exists whether, in its range and quality, administrative action will prove equal to the responsibilities assumed by the central and state governments in the Second Five-Year Plan.'

This doubt about administrative constraints proved valid. Thus, the Third Five-Year Plan (1961) highlighted that the administrative machinery had been strained and, at many points in the structure, the available personnel were not adequate in quality and numbers. It was also lucid in recognizing that the expansion of administrative responsibilities was itself an important cause of inefficiency and delay. As large burdens were thrown on the administrative structure, it grew in size—and as its size increased, it became slower in its functioning. Delays occurred and affected operations at every stage, and the expected outputs were further deferred.

Another lacuna in the old strategy was the absence of a link between priorities and policies. The priorities were clear, but the instruments chosen to achieve these priorities failed to deliver. A command-type planning, based on the Soviet model, proved unsuitable for directing investments in an economy that was largely privately owned and where the judicial and legal framework guaranteed freedom of choice to individuals. The system of direct control and physical allocation, which was essentially derived from provisions introduced during the Second World War, proved more successful in preventing competition than in directing investments according to clear priorities. There was a dichotomy between physical production targets as set out in the Third Five-Year Plan, and the framework of macroeconomic policies—particularly tariff and fiscal policies. The earlier Plans assigned an important role to the fiscal system to bring about a better distribution of income; yet, the ratio of direct taxes in national income actually went down over the years. Agriculture enjoyed a high priority, but agriculture exports were discouraged or banned altogether, which resulted in a reduction in farmers' incomes. The Plans encouraged import substitution to reduce import dependence, but industrial and tariff policies encouraged domestic manufacture for the domestic market, based on imports of components and raw materials.

The debate on economic policy in the 1980s also naturally focused on whether the strategy of development adopted after Independence was right, and the effect of this strategy on India's economic development. This strategy, which was greatly influenced by the Soviet planning model, gave a central role to the state in the control and direction of economic activity. Following the Soviet experience, it was believed that the savings rate in the economy as well as the growth rate could be increased if India invested heavily in the capital-goods and heavy-industry sectors, at the expense of the consumer-goods sector. Since the investment requirements in these sectors were high, largely beyond the capability of the private sector, and the financial profitability was low, it followed that such investments would have to be undertaken by the state.

The state emerged both as the mobilizer of savings as well as an important investor and owner of capital. Since the state was to be the primary agent of economic change, it followed that private-sector activities had to be strictly regulated and controlled to conform to the objectives of state policy.

In this scheme foreign trade had a relatively small role, partly because of the belief that trade was biased against developing countries and primary producers, and partly because of the intellectual conviction that export prospects were severely limited. India's First Five-Year Plan (1951) was practically silent on exports. It only highlighted the limitations to prospects of increasing export earnings since 'the prices obtainable for exports depend on world factors and may, therefore, be subject to large variations'. The Second Five-Year Plan (1956) attempted a projection of balance of trade, but concluded that no significant increase in export earnings in the short run could be expected. The intellectual basis for pessimism about exports, which was widely shared by development economists of the time, was broadly the same as that articulated by Nurkse in his 'export lag' thesis. In the famous Wicksell Lectures (1961), Nurkse drew attention to the tendency of the exports of primary producing countries to lag behind the rate of increase in international trade in general and of the trade between and from industrial countries.[1]

The primacy accorded to capital accumulation by the state also meant that, in the early years of planning, there was a relative neglect of public investment in agriculture. This neglect of agriculture was supported by the prevailing view that a growing labour force in developing countries could only be absorbed in industry, and that in the early stages of industrialization it was necessary for agriculture to contribute to the building up of modern industry by providing cheap labour. A faster development of the industrial sector was the central objective of planning.

So far as actual performance of the economy in the 1980s is concerned, the main highlights are easy to recapitulate. There is little doubt that the rate of growth of the Indian economy in the post-Independence period was substantially higher than that registered by the country in the last hundred years. It is estimated that the rate of growth of the Indian economy between 1871 and 1946 was barely enough to keep pace with the growth of population. The rate of growth during 1951–84 was about 3.8 per cent per annum, which slightly increased to 4 per cent by 1989–90. (The actual number may vary, depending on the treatment of drought years and the statistical method used for calculation.) This rate of growth was, however, lower than that of developing countries as a group (5.2 per cent). It was also substantially lower than that registered by China (5.4 per cent) and several other developing countries, such as South Korea (7.2 per cent), Taiwan (9.1 per cent), Thailand (6.8 per cent), Indonesia (5.5 per cent) and Malaysia (6 per cent). The per capita income growth in India was less than 2 per cent per annum during the four decades after Independence. Population grew at 2.15 per cent per annum, as compared to 1.21 per cent per annum in the preceding three decades. This largely offset the benefit of higher growth in the post-Independence period.

Despite the central role accorded to industrial development in India's planning, industrial growth was 5.3 per cent per annum from the early 1950s to the early 1980s. The share of the industrial sector in the GDP (gross domestic product) increased from 15 to 23 per cent over the whole period, but its share of the labour force rose only from 12.6 to 13.8 per cent. The deceleration in the growth rate of industry since the mid-1960s (up to 1980–81) was particularly striking. The annual growth rate of GDP in the manufacturing sector declined from 7.4 per cent, before the drought years of the mid-1960s, to only 4.3 per cent between 1967–68 and 1980–81. The growth of agricultural output was also slow. The annual growth of income of agriculture between 1950–51 to 1984–85 was 2.12 per cent per annum, while the per capita agricultural income hardly increased. This is comparable to China, but is much less than the numbers achieved in some other developing countries. The growth rate in agriculture, particularly food output, was barely ahead of the population growth.

India's export performance was also relatively poor, and the country failed to take advantage of the expansion of world trade in the post-war period. In the 1950s there was a virtual stagnation of exports; they grew somewhat faster at the rate of 3.3 per cent annually in the 1960s, rising to 7.5 per cent per annum in the 1970s. India's exports were 7.8 per cent of the GDP in 1980–81, which was virtually the same in 1950–51. On the other hand, the share of exports in the GDP of developing countries, as a group, increased from 15 per cent of their GDP, in 1960, to 22 per cent. The fall in India's share of world trade was even more dramatic: it fell from 2.4 per cent at the time of Independence to only 0.4 per cent in the 1980s.

Except for a brief period, India experienced continuing balance-of-payments problems, which made economic management and planning extremely difficult. Bureaucratic controls proliferated, leading to excessive delays in the approval and implementation of projects, and to an increase in the cost of investment. The capital-output ratio increased significantly. The incremental capital-output ratio increased from 3.89 and 5.46 in the 1950s and 1960s, respectively, to 6.04 in the 1970s. A part of this increase was due to structural shifts in the investment pattern, but a significant part was also due to lower productivity and higher capital intensity.

Critics of India's performance in the 1980s also drew attention to the fact that India's record in health, education and other social indicators had similarly remained far from satisfactory. According to the 1990 Human Development Report of the United Nations, India ranked low on the human development index (with an index value of only 0.44, compared to China's 0.72 and South Korea's 0.90). In India, the reduction in the under-five infant mortality rate was 2.3 per cent per annum during 1960–88, as against 5.4 per cent per annum in China and 4.5 per cent per annum in South Korea. In 1985, the adult literacy rate in India was only 43 per cent, compared to 69 per cent in China. (South Korea's literacy rate was already high in 1970, at 88 per cent; it is likely that illiteracy was eliminated by 1985). As for poverty levels, according to Planning Commission calculations, there was a reduction in the percentage of people living below the poverty line, from about 50 per cent in 1972–73 to about 30 per cent in 1987–88. The absolute number of the poor in the mid-1980s, however, remained over 270 million.

It may be recalled that there was remarkable unanimity, in the 1940s and 1950s, among the pioneers of development economics on the proposition that industrialization was synonymous with development, and that industrialization was not feasible in underdeveloped economies without an active role assigned to the state. Thus, on the basis of the time-series data on the national products of different countries, Kuznets (1955)[2] showed that the process of economic development was always accompanied by a shift in the labour force from low-productivity agriculture to high-productivity manufacturing. Such a shift required a higher degree of capital accumulation. Rosenstein-Rodan (1943)[3] argued that the production process in modern industry was subject to indivisibilities and economies of scale. This required large investments in social overhead capital areas, such as transport, communications, power and urban infrastructure. Such investments could only be forthcoming if the state played an active role in mobilizing and investing social resources. Scitovsky (1954)[4] pointed to the limitations of a price-guided system in taking advantage of external economies. The implication was that the market mechanism could be relied on to take care of the production problem in the economy, but investment allocation required state intervention.

The early development literature was also sanguine about the need for the state to exercise its regulatory and fiscal powers to alter colonial patterns of trade. The conclusions of Prebisch (1950)[5]—on the secular tendency of the terms of trade turning against countries exporting primary products and importing manufacturers—had an important impact on the thinking of planners in developing countries. Prebisch and Singer attributed the tendency of the terms of trade of primary producers to decline to the power of trade unions in advanced countries and to conditions of underemployment in the periphery. Equally influential was Lewis's paper on the implications for development strategy of 'unlimited supply of labour' (Lewis, 1954).[6] Lewis argued that under the conditions of an unlimited supply of labour, the gains from productivity increases in the export sector were likely to accrue to importing countries.

These perceptions of eminent economists were widely shared by political leaders and Indian intellectuals of the time, and the business of choosing an economic strategy responded to these perceptions. The neglect of economic development by the state in the colonial period had an inevitable consequence. The conviction grew that development was not possible without the guiding hand of the state: the state was required to take on the role of planner, saver, investor and manager in order to quicken the pace of development. The trade regime in India was free for about a century but this did not result in growth or prosperity. There was practically no industry or diversification of trade, and the country was heavily dependent on imports of manufactures. It is striking that, as late as 1830, India's share of world manufacturing output was 17.6 per cent, compared to the UK's share of 9.5 per cent and the United States' share of 2.4 per cent. By 1900, however, India's share had dwindled to 1.7 per cent, compared to the UK's share of 18.5 per cent and the United States' share of 23.6 per cent (Kennedy, 1989).[7]

The colonial experience was sufficient to reinforce the belief that the free-trade regime was biased against India and other developing countries and thus could not be relied upon to generate growth and improve living standards. The call for Swadeshi, therefore, became an important element in the political struggle against colonial rule. It was inevitable that, after Independence, the building of an indigenous manufacturing base would become an important objective of economic policy. This strategy was also an aspect of the struggle for economic and political independence from the UK and other Western powers. The apparent success of the Soviet Union in building a strong manufacturing base, coupled with its emergence as a superpower within a relatively short period of time, strengthened belief in the efficacy of the state as the primary agent of accumulation.

The post-Independence period in India was characterized by several external and domestic shocks, such as war, drought, oil-price increases and political upheaval. In defence of the earlier Indian strategy, it can be argued that while the growth rate was slower, India was able to maintain a stable and democratic political system with a mixed economy against very difficult odds. This was a unique achievement in the developing world. The nation was able to achieve self-sufficiency in food. India was also able to develop a diversified industrial structure and raise its savings rate, from 10 per cent of the GDP in 1950–51 to 21 per cent in the mid-1980s.

The debate on what could have been possible if a different path had been chosen can go on endlessly. Fortunately, it is not necessary to settle this debate in order to consider what India *should* do in the future. The choices made in the early stages of development depended on the opportunities and the knowledge available then. In addition, it cannot be argued with any degree of confidence that if an alternative strategy were chosen, the aggregate and long-term results would have been more favourable throughout the post-Independence period. Perhaps the growth rate would have been higher for a while, but the economy could have become more dependent and been unable to cope with the weight of adverse external developments—as indeed was the case in the 1980s, when there was some shift in the strategy.

It thus seems that the initial choice of India's economic strategy is understandable within the particular economic and political context in which this choice was made. However, it is also necessary to recognize the drawbacks and weaknesses of the strategy as it evolved over the forty years after Independence.

By the 1960s, it had become clear that the domestic and international context was rapidly changing and the economy was facing a new set of internal and external challenges that could not have been visualized at the beginning of the Planning era. In fact, the failure on the external front had already become evident by 1958, when the Plan and the economy had to be rescued through a massive international aid effort. Internally, the aftermath of increased defence expenditures resulting from the 1962 war with China and the two wars with Pakistan led to the emergence of a fiscal problem and to a slowdown in the rate of growth of public investment—which was supposed to be the engine of industrial growth. The devastating droughts of 1965–67 and India's dependence on food imports from the United States underlined the weakness of the agricultural strategy. It is a fair criticism of India's post-Independence development strategy that the country's economic policy was unresponsive to changing internal and external circumstances. India failed to adapt rapidly and sufficiently to changing circumstances, wherein the industrial economy became more complex, and was not responsive enough as the international environment changed from the relatively stable period of the 1950s and early 1960s to an environment characterized by rapid change.

It was also clear that a command-type planning, as developed in the Soviet Union, could not work effectively in an economy that was mostly privately run and where producers and consumers had the freedom of choice when it came to making economic decisions. The legal and judicial framework was also such that the power of the state to enforce economic decisions was severely hamstrung. The instruments of planning relied heavily on administrative and physical control. The state took on too much in too many areas, and in too much painstaking detail. This vast playground, like Hamlet's Denmark, was becoming impossible to manage or administer. Limitations in administrative resources and capability became important constraints to development.

A conspicuous failure, particularly in the 1980s, was the inability of the fiscal system to generate sufficient real resources for investment and capital formation. An important assumption in the choice of strategy was the primary role assigned to the public sector for increasing savings in the economy. It was assumed that the propensity to save out of incomes in the public sector would be higher than that in the private sector. Actual experience belied this expectation. While revenues generally increased in line with plan targets, public savings tended to decline, leading to an insufficiency of resources for public investment.

India's Plans failed to develop a viable strategy for the management of balance of payments. Since 1956–57, except for a few years, the balance-of-payments problem merely varied in its intensity. The Plans overemphasized the import substitution of finished products, and insufficient attention was paid to interlinkages among the various sectors and to the impact of the tariff regime in encouraging an import-intensive input structure. There was an underestimation of the economy's import requirements of industrial raw materials (for example, metals and chemicals, petroleum products, fertilizers and sophisticated capital goods).

In the light of India's own experience and findings of theoretical and empirical research in 1990, a programme of action that could lay the foundations of sustainable growth in the 1990s, and which could be implemented quickly, was highlighted by several critics of India's planning process in the 1990s. Among these were:

1. *Foreign Exchange*: India's experience in the 1980s amply demonstrated the vulnerability of the economy to external shocks, and the underlying weakness of India's balance of payments. The likely emergence of a severe balance-of-payments problem was long anticipated, but remedial measures could not be taken because of domestic political developments since 1988. The cost to the economy was heavy. The most pressing priority

then was to take measures to reduce the trade deficit to more manageable levels. There was sufficient evidence to show that India's incentive structure was heavily weighted in favour of domestic sales, while being biased against exports. Such import liberalization as had occurred was 'inward-looking', and promoted imports of non-competing raw materials, components and capital goods for domestic manufacture for the domestic market. In the mid-1980s, an attempt was initiated to shift the balance of advantage in favour of exports. It was suggested that this process had to go much further and, in addition to other structural reforms, an explicit market-based link had to be established between exports and imports. There is also no option but to restrain the growth of imports of crude oil, petroleum products and fertilizers. This has to be done by a combination of measures on the demand and supply sides. Until such time as a better balance can be achieved on the trade account, the country has no option but to manage with shortages of these products, if necessary. This would be economically less costly than borrowing more and more to pay for current consumption.

2. *Public Debt*: Several studies had already established, beyond doubt, the alarming profile of India's growing public debt, including its external debt. India had been borrowing, both internally and externally, to finance widening deficits in its revenue and capital accounts. This process cannot be carried much further without landing the country in a financial disaster. There is enough empirical evidence from the history of other countries to show that high inflation, including the possibility of hyperinflation, lay ahead if the situation

was not stabilized soon. India's external debt, in terms of gross national product (GNP), was relatively low in the 1980s as compared to that of heavily indebted countries in Latin America and elsewhere. However, in relation to exports, the size of the debt has already reached Latin American proportions. The rate of growth of external debt, therefore, needs to be reduced and kept well below the rate of growth of exports, so that the debt/export ratio is brought down significantly over the next few years.

3. *Fiscal deficit*: A proper management of public debt as well as the balance of payments requires firm action to reduce fiscal deficits. A medium-term objective, therefore, is to eliminate the revenue deficit altogether, so that the government does not need to borrow in order to finance current expenditure. The need to control expenditure has already been felt by the government for some time, but, for political economy reasons, it has not been considered feasible to make much progress. In a multiparty democracy like India, experience shows that nothing short of a constitutional amendment, which is binding on all governments—present and future—would be effective in eliminating revenue deficits. In addition to expenditure control, measures to widen the tax base, simplify the tax system and improve the revenue administration are also important elements in a programme meant to reduce budget deficits. It is, therefore, suggested that a more transparent system with uniform rules and less product differentiation would increase the buoyancy of the tax system.

4. *The Public Sector*: The management of the public sector is also a key issue. In view of its large size, a sustained improvement in the savings available for investment is

not likely to be feasible without higher productivity. As the size of the capital market in India in 1990 was only about 1 per cent of the value of the total assets of the public sector (at historical cost), it is clear that a wholesale privatization of public-sector units was not a feasible option in the Indian situation in the foreseeable future. It is, therefore, suggested that all commercial enterprises should be required to raise equity and loans for their further growth from financial and capital markets. Sick units and smaller units with low profitability may be sold through public offers. Beyond these measures, the solutions to the problems of the public sector in India would have to be found primarily within the framework of public ownership. In addition to streamlining the administration and a proper management of the public sector, it is now also necessary to impose a 'hard budget' constraint on the public sector. Central and state governments should be prohibited, by law, from financing the losses of public-sector units. It does not make sense for the government to borrow at a high cost to finance public-sector losses as well as its own revenue deficits. In this respect, the situation in the 1990s is fundamentally different from that prevailing in the 1960s or 1970s, when the revenue budget was in surplus. It is, therefore, suggested that, henceforth, public-sector units should depend on existing banking and financial mechanisms to meet their credit requirements, in accordance with normal policy. A hard budget constraint is not only a means of saving revenue for government but also an important instrument for inducing 'productive' efficiency. Public-sector enterprises need to be reorganized along competitive lines.

5. *Competition*: Cross-country research as well as industry-level studies have shown that a competitive environment is crucial for promoting efficiency in resource use and allocation in the economy. In the earlier era, the industrial licensing system and macroeconomic policies (including fiscal policy) had prevented competitive inducements to efficiency. This has to be reversed. The capacity-based industrial licensing system needs to be abolished. Fiscal, financial and tariff policies should be used to provide the necessary signals for resource allocation. In view of external financing difficulties, import liberalization (which raises the import-to-GDP ratio), while desirable, may not be a feasible option right now. However, the rates of effective protection for inefficient domestic manufacturing can be reduced by moving towards more uniform tariffs across industries (in respect of both inputs and outputs). There is also a need for simplification, transparency and uniformity in import policy. The tariff system should cease to be cost-based, and no financial subsidies or credit concessions should be provided to support inefficient and non-competitive production.

6. *Controls*: The system of physical and discretionary controls, inherited from the Second World War, has certainly outlived its utility. These methods have proved much less efficient than what was once assumed in directing economic activity to desired channels and optimizing the use of resources. In view of administrative constraints and information gaps, such controls have failed to cope with the rapidly changing technological and international environment. They have also given rise to corruption and economically wasteful activities, such as rent-seeking. Direct physical controls on production

and international trade should, therefore, be replaced by non-discretionary fiscal, credit and financial controls. This would improve the quality of state intervention and make it more effective. This has been the experience of several other highly interventionist but economically successful countries, such as Japan and South Korea. Several government committees have already recommended a shift to non-discretionary methods of state intervention, but the actual progress has been negligible.

7. *Decentralization*: This is both a political and an economic necessity. Politically, with the emergence of strong regional parties, and with several different parties in power at the Centre and states, the decentralization of state power has become necessary. Decentralization also has the incidental advantage of reducing the power of dominant coalitions at the Centre by creating several competing power bases. Action at two levels is necessary; the planning and financing of activities, which are the responsibility of state governments (such as investments in rural development, education and social services), should be transferred from the Centre to the states, and the states, in turn, should transfer the responsibility for local area planning to local institutions. Past experience does not show that centralized or higher-level planning in these areas lead to better and more efficient planning. The decision-making process in respect of the public sector, including financial institutions, needs to be decentralized from government secretariats to enterprises.

8. *Literacy*: The importance of literacy—both as an end in itself and as a means of raising the growth rate of output—has long been recognized in economic literature. India's overall record in this area so far leaves much to

be desired. One outstanding example of the successful implementation of the literacy programme was Kerala, where the literacy ratio reached 91 per cent in 1990, according to the census. Kerala's example showed that full literacy is an achievable goal even in a poor country, and that techniques to reach this goal are available (for instance, through mass literacy campaigns). There is also evidence to show that high literacy rates—especially high female literacy rates—are associated with low rates of population growth, which is an important development objective for India. In Kerala, higher literacy rates resulted in a lower-than-average rate of population growth (1.31 per cent per annum by 1990 compared to the average of 2.11 per cent for India). Higher literacy rates were also associated with better performance in terms of a number of other health and social indicators, such as infant mortality rates. On the other hand, in various states, such as Madhya Pradesh, Rajasthan and Uttar Pradesh, abysmally low literacy rates have been associated with higher-than-average population growth rates and poor performance in terms of health indicators. It was suggested that full literacy should be the national development goal of the 1990s—just as self-sufficiency in food was the dominant objective of national planning after the disastrous droughts of 1965–67.

9. *Food and poverty*: It should be explicitly recognized that a programme of fiscal and balance-of-payments correction would impose social costs. Experience also shows that, unless compensatory policies are put in place, a reduction in domestic absorption generally affects the poor more than the better-off sections of society. However, as it happens, expenditure cuts are generally more severe on

social sectors than on the administration or industrial sectors. It is easier to cut expenditure on, say, new schools or new hospitals that have not yet been established than on lumpy investments in industrial plants that are still in the process of implementation. The interests of, and power enjoyed by, organized lobbies is also greater in respect of the latter sort of projects. It is important that the strategy to reduce fiscal deficits in India does not neglect this aspect. Food subsidies should continue to be maintained. A part of the revenue gain from the reduction of other subsidies and the higher recovery of costs should be used to expand rural employment programmes.

10. *Administration*: Both in India and elsewhere, in the post-Independence period, widespread intervention by the state was considered necessary to alter colonial patterns of production and trade. The results were generally beneficial as growth rates accelerated, and progress was achieved in reducing the incidence of poverty. However, over time, in response to various pressures and needs, the state has expanded in all directions. The overextension of the state has become a problem, outstripping available managerial and administrative capacities. The economic costs of delays and the overlapping of functions have been enormous, and these have been recognized by India's Plans since the early 1970s. The vast expansion of the state has also given rise to the emergence of various types of lobbies and coalitions that erode the capacity of the state to intervene autonomously in the interests of society as a whole. It is clear that an important priority of the 1990s was to reduce the size of the state and make the administrative apparatus more functional. The latter

objective may not be realized unless the area of the state activity is reduced at all levels and confined to what is socially necessary and beneficial.

These are a selective list of priorities. It is likely that if India succeeded in the early 1990s in implementing the programme suggested above, all else would become easier to accomplish in the near future. The way ahead is difficult, but it is also full of promise and opportunity. India's difficulty in the preceding years must not be allowed to overshadow the considerable achievements of the past nor dim the vision of the future.

2

Controls, Regulations and the State[*]

Over time, in the post-Independence era, India accumulated a plethora of economic and social legislations for regulating all aspects of human behaviour. The objectives of most of these legislations were generally highly laudable as they were designed to cover a perceived social or economic need. However, on the ground, the complex web of laws and regulations could not be enforced in practice. The problem of effective implementation was complicated by legal and procedural hassles. The non-enforcement of existing laws had some important economic consequences. It made non-compliance and illegal activity more profitable than legal activity. This had the further consequence of distorting product and capital markets to the point where unproductive and rent-seeking activities could be more rewarding than the production of real commodities and services.

---

[*] Edited version of Chapter 1 of *India's Economic Policy: Preparing for the Twenty-First Century* (New Delhi: Penguin, 1996).

The Urban Land Ceilings Act (1976) and the long-standing rent-control laws vividly illustrate the strong economic incentives that such laws provided for unproductive and speculative activities. These laws had excellent social objectives. These included releasing vacant land for construction of houses, reducing the concentration of wealth and protecting poor tenants. However, over time, the actual results were the opposite. Housing construction virtually stopped in metropolitan towns, rents soared and property values multiplied. As rental agreements could not be legally enforced within a reasonable period, illegal cash transactions were widespread and the market for housing became non-functional. The poor and the low-wage earners were the worst affected as their effective rents multiplied and the supply of low-cost housing diminished.

India was meant to be a federation of states. However, to facilitate planning, the power to regulate, direct and undertake economic activities came to be centralized in the Union government. Over time, there has been a vast expansion of the Central government, which now has nearly 3.5 million employees. This compares with a total employment of about 4.5 million persons in manufacturing in the private organized sector.[1] The number of ministries and departments has also proliferated. At the same time, state governments continue to be vested with the primary responsibility for development activities in all sectors including infrastructure (for instance, roads and power), industry, social sectors (particularly health and education), agriculture and poverty alleviation. State governments have also expanded enormously. The expansion of Central and state governments has created a multiplicity of problems, not the least of which are increases in transaction costs of economic activities and the heavy budgetary burden of salaries and pensions.

An interesting feature of the control regime that dominated the Indian economy for nearly four decades was that it was virtually indistinguishable from the system of controls over production, distribution and allocation of resources prevalent during the Second World War. Thus, some of the main instruments of economic legislation—the Foreign Exchange Regulation Act, the Imports and Exports (Controls) Act, the Industries (Development and Regulation) Act and the Essential Commodities Act—could be traced to the wartime Defence of India Act or to the Statement of Industrial Policy in 1945. These instruments fitted well with the Soviet model of economic planning introduced in India after Independence. They were, therefore, continued as well as expanded to meet certain other social and economic goals.

The expansion of the government's role in practically all spheres of the economy since Independence occurred gradually and haphazardly in response to new problems and political compulsions. Each step had a logic of its own, but due consideration was not given to their cumulative impact on the economy. Thus, in the 1950s, since savings and incomes were low, it seemed natural for the government to take on the task of mobilizing incremental savings through taxation and market borrowings. The base of entrepreneurship, as in many other developing countries, was small and concentrated in some regions of the country. The large investments required in the steel and machine-building sectors could only be undertaken directly by the government in view of the underdeveloped financial sector. By the end of the 1960s, the concentration of economic power in a few business houses had become a major political and economic issue; this further strengthened the role of the state in the industrial sphere. Banks were nationalized in order to break the nexus between private industry and finance, and to make credit available to the traditionally underfunded sectors, such as agriculture and small-scale industries.

As the government's own need for resources for investment increased, it became necessary to curb or control the private sector's demand for resources through the rationing of foreign exchange, credit controls and industrial licensing. The action to ration and the allocation of scarce resources added to the complexity of rules and regulations and increased the scope for the exercise of administrative discretion. As requirements got larger and resources became smaller, the administrative process had to embrace more functions in view of the linkages among different sectors.

As several scholars have argued, the initial choice of development strategy, which gave a central role to the state in the control and direction of economic activity, was entirely understandable within the particular economic and political context in which this choice was made.[2] The neglect of economic development during the colonial period was too deep and had persisted for too long to permit any other outcome. For a while, the actual results in terms of industrial development and economic growth were quite good, at least by historical standards. Spurred by large public investments and protected markets, industrial growth in the 1950s and early 1960s was close to 8 per cent per annum. The growth of overall national income during this period was about 3.5 per cent per annum, which was lower than expected, but still considerably higher than that registered by the country in the last hundred years. India's investment rate also went up, and, what was more, most of it was financed from domestic savings.

However, the strategy and the accompanying control system ran out of steam by the mid-1960s and proved incapable of coping with external shocks and responding adequately to the rapidly changing domestic and international circumstances. Between 1965 and 1980, industrial growth slowed down considerably, and foreign-exchange shortages became chronic. The public sector, instead of contributing to growth of savings in the economy, became a drain on resources. Growth in factory employment was less than the increase in the urban labour force. There was practically no reduction in the burden of rural underemployment. Per capita incomes in the rural sector in 1980 were about the same as in 1960. India's record in health, education and other social indicators, too, was unsatisfactory. While there was some improvement, the pace of change was well below India's own requirements and that of the record of other countries.

With the benefit of hindsight, it is now clear that, after the initial phase of import-substitution, some of the basic assumptions underlying India's development strategy simply proved to be wrong. Unrealistic assumptions about the impact of the import-substitution strategy on the economy's import requirements also led to a relative neglect of exports. This resulted in the growing current-account deficits, which became difficult to finance.

Jobs, Wages and Trade

It is not surprising that a control system that was designed to meet the requirements of the first half of the twentieth century or of the Second World War effectively failed to meet the challenges of the latter half of the century. By 1990, the global economy was characterized by unprecedented technological change as well as significant changes in trade patterns and political relations between industrialized and developing countries. In fact, the primary characteristics that were used to determine the classification of countries as industrialized or primary producing (such as the degree of industrialization or the share of trade in manufacturing) were no longer valid. Consider, for example the following:

- The share of manufacturers in developing-country exports actually rose from 20 per cent to 60 per cent between 1960 and 1990. Low- and middle-income countries accounted for almost 80 per cent of the world's industrial workforce. What was even more striking was that, contrary to conventional thinking, the developing countries' share of the world's skilled workforce also jumped from a third to nearly a half. By 1990, the industrialized countries no longer had a monopoly of manufacturing production, while developing countries were no longer exclusively dependent on low-value trade in primary products.

- A fast growth in manufacturing was associated with a high rate of increase in employment and wages of workers. For example, manufacturing wages in East Asia rose by 270 per cent in real terms between 1970 and 1990, while manufacturing employment increased by 500 per cent. In India, however, wage employment in industry grew by only about 50 per cent during this period, and real wages in the organized sector increased by about the same amount.

- Higher growth in manufacturing resulted in the movement of workers from low-wage agriculture and plantations to high-wage manufacturing jobs. In Malaysia, for example, one in two employees worked on plantations in 1957. As a result of the high industrial growth since then, by 1990, only one in ten workers was engaged in plantation agriculture. Wage employment tripled between 1957 and 1989, while the share of the workforce employed in agriculture fell from 58 per cent to 26 per cent.

• Earlier, it was believed that the private sector did not have the resources to invest in capital-intensive large industry. By 1990, however, the bulk of investment in developing countries in infrastructure, capital-intensive and long-gestation projects came from the private sector, not the public sector.

A number of factors account for why the developing countries, by 1990, emerged as the major producers and exporters of manufactured goods in the global economy. First and foremost, the end of the colonial rule and participation by developing countries in post–Second World War trade negotiations significantly levelled the international playing fields. Unlike the earlier periods of globalization in the late nineteenth and the early twentieth centuries, the trading pattern among different groups of countries, with some exceptions, reflected the real comparative advantage among nations. The interventionist strategies during the early years of the postcolonial period helped to establish an industrial base and an industrial culture in many developing countries, which could be used to exploit the new opportunities in international trade in the 1970s and 1980s. This process was helped enormously by changes in the direction of foreign investment. Up to the end of the Second World War, foreign investment was entirely directed towards the production and trade of primary products (for example, plantations, minerals and oil). By 1990, the bulk of foreign investment had gone into manufacturing and service industries.

Another important factor that helped the growth of developing countries' trade in manufacturing was the cost-reducing technological change between 1960 and 1990. Technological change made the accumulation of 'skills' a more important factor in determining comparative advantage than capital endowments. Developing countries that benefited the most from technological change were also the ones where the level of skill formation and education was high, as in countries in East Asia and China. Finally, the sharp decline in costs of communication and transport made geography and proximity to markets less relevant in influencing the choice of location for manufacturing.

The above changes enabled the developing countries to play a more decisive role in international trade. The extent to which different countries and regions benefited from these trends, of course, depended on individual country policies and their overall economic performance. Initial endowments and initial conditions (particularly in respect of education and health) also played a role, but these too were amenable to change.

Some critics drew attention to certain legitimate concerns about the impact of developments in trade, technology and investment on the prospects of poorer developing countries.[3] These concerns centred around two possible effects. First, as domestic production became dependent on global markets, it also became increasingly less attached to the particular interests and values of its country of origin. As domestic and foreign companies competed against rival firms for world-market shares, they became more vulnerable to shifts in comparative advantage or changes in labour market conditions. If, for example, wages rose during a period of high growth, plants and jobs moved elsewhere. Second, countries became more vulnerable to the instability associated with international capital flows. Developing countries had less institutional control over such flows and were thus not able to cope with the economic consequences of financial instability. Further, while countries in East Asia and Latin America benefited from the above developments because of their high levels of literacy and development, similar opportunities were not available for countries in South Asia and Africa in the 1980s. India's participation in trade in 1990 was less than 0.5 per cent, while the share of foreign capital was even less. Compared with other poor countries, India also had a large pool of industrial and technical manpower. Although firm statistics are not available, it is likely that during this period, India was a *net* supplier of managerial and professional personnel to the rest of the world. In other words, a larger number of persons of Indian origin were working in managerial positions in foreign companies abroad than the number of foreigners working in the same positions in India.

The Role of Government

In the 1980s, there were some important changes in the domestic political and economic situation in India, as indeed in several other developing countries with large public sectors and overextended governments. Economically, because of fiscal profligacy, the state became financially weak, with little command over resources for investment in capital formation or programmes for the poor. The revenue surpluses of the earlier years disappeared, and the state and the public sector were heavily in debt. Politically, as governments became overextended, there were signs of decline in what political scientists have referred to as the 'authority' of the state.[4] These were evident in the deteriorating law-and-order situation in several parts of the country, the increasing appeal of regionalism and subnationalism, tensions between the Centre and its constituent parts, decline in the quality of public services, inordinate delays and cost overruns in public projects and the increasing failure of policies and plans to deliver what had been promised.

As it happened, over the years, it became evident that even the simplest administrative functions were not being performed, or were performed only after long delays and cost overruns. A prime example of administrative hurdles to efficient operations was the inability to fill top-level vacancies in the public sector. Such appointments were entirely within the purview of the government and were not subject to external control, such as trade union pressures or parliamentary scrutiny. Yet, the task was not performed, resulting in enormous inefficiencies and further financial losses. The system, as a whole, became dysfunctional and unresponsive to the needs of a modern society.

If one reflects on the profound changes that have taken place in all aspects of national life and the international economy, the conclusion is inescapable—the system of controls and regulations enabling state control of economic activity, devised in India during the Second World War, should have been abandoned on a wholesale basis soon after

Independence. The old system should have been replaced with an altogether new system—of the public surveillance of private economic activity by individuals, associations and corporations.

Governments and Markets

It must be stressed that the above conclusion has very little to do with ideology, or the theoretical superiority or otherwise of markets over governments. In real life, there is no such thing as a perfect market or a perfect government. Nor is there any evidence to support the notion of 'good markets and bad governments' or the opposite ('bad markets and good governments'). Both governments and markets are necessary in the real world, and both can be good or bad in a particular country in a specific situation. In India's case, in the light of developments that took place twenty years or so after Independence, it was necessary to redefine the relative roles of the market and the government. The government, which had become overextended, needed to intervene less. Markets, which were monopolistic and protected, should have become more open.

The elimination of ineffective and counterproductive controls was, of course, not easy in view of the power of vested interests and political resistance to 'rocking the boat'. As a first practical step, all new productive activities or new projects could be exempted from the scope of restrictive economic legislation. For example, an exemption from rent-control laws could be provided for new construction, an exemption from the Urban Ceiling Act could be provided for urban land that has not yet been acquired, an exemption from employment-restrictive labour laws could be provided for new employees, an exemption from the Foreign Exchange

Regulation Act (FERA) could be provided for new capital investment, and so on. As a next step, an all-party committee of Parliament and each of the state legislatures should be asked to review all economic and social legislations, not in terms of their objectives, but in terms of the actual quantifiable criteria (for instance, the trend in property values or growth in manufacturing employment) rather than vague generalizations regarding the contribution of controls to social goals.

The relative roles of the Central and state governments in the economy should also be redefined. The Central government should withdraw altogether from implementation, or from having any role to play in the monitoring or direction of economic programmes in all spheres. The main role of the Centre should be the management of macroeconomic policy and the definition and enforcement of the legal framework for economic activities, including the movement of goods, services and people across state boundaries. The implementation of economic programmes should be the responsibility of state governments. The system of financial transfers between the Centre and the states, despite some drawbacks, has worked reasonably well over the years without being overly contentious. Not much is to be gained by reopening well-established conventions and rules regarding the division of financial powers between the Centre and states.

Even after cleaning up the accumulated mess of the past, the Central and state governments have a lot to do. The Central government has primary responsibility for tax collection, setting the fiscal agenda, managing foreign trade, external economic relations, the interstate planning of physical infrastructure, transport and communication policy, the development of the financial sector, monetary and credit policies (along with the Reserve Bank of India), environment and resettlement policies, and so on. State governments are majorly entrusted with the implementation of economic and social programmes for the improvement of their cities and villages and for the betterment of the people living there. The need for a vigorous programme to improve the physical infrastructure and to expand the reach of primary education and basic healthcare is also urgent. If governments do more of what they alone can do (like, provide access to primary education or health services for the poor, and enable the development of public infrastructure) and less of what they cannot do, the country would benefit greatly.

3

After the Crisis: Need for a New Strategy

The seven-year period from 1984–85 to 1990–91 was marked by a high rate of industrial growth. The overall index of industrial production grew by 8.5 per cent per annum and the manufacturing sector grew by 9 per cent per annum during this period. A steady growth rate of this order over a fairly long period was achieved after a gap of two decades. Contrary to popular belief, industrial growth was fairly widespread and not concentrated only in certain sectors such as automobiles, electronics and consumer durables. These sectors did register very impressive growth, but their contribution to the overall growth rate of industrial production was relatively modest, because they did not hold a large weight in the index. During the 1980s, in the overall growth of industrial production, nearly 47 per cent was accounted for by basic goods, 21 per cent by capital goods, 16 per cent by intermediate goods, and only 7 per cent by durable consumption goods and 9 per cent by non-durable consumption goods.

During 1991–92, however, the index of industrial production was practically stationary, and there was no growth in overall industrial production. There was a significant increase in the output of several infrastructure industries, such as electricity and coal, but this was more than offset by a decline in manufacturing production. The production of manufacturing industries fell by about 1.8 per cent in 1991–92. Within the manufacturing sector, the sharpest decline occurred in the production of capital goods. This sector, which had shown high rates of growth in the 1980s, registered a decline of 17 per cent. The other industrial group that showed a similar decline in production was consumer durables, in which output declined by about 14 per cent.

The turning point in manufacturing production appears to have occurred in April 1991. Until then, despite the adverse effects of the Gulf crisis in the second half of 1990–91 and a host of domestic uncertainties, manufacturing production had continued to increase. The adverse impact of severe import-compression measures introduced after the Gulf crisis on output appeared to have been deferred somewhat, and the initial adjustment affected inventories more than output. At that time, the expectation was that the Gulf crisis would not last long, and that import-compression measures could be withdrawn quickly. The Gulf crisis did indeed last for only about six months, but in India's case, the adverse effects were compounded because of political uncertainty. In addition to the direct effects of an increase in oil prices on the balance of payments, India also faced a 'liquidity squeeze' because of the withdrawal of deposits by non-resident Indians (NRIs) and the cessation of lending by commercial banks. As a result, the import-compression measures became even more severe, which naturally affected the growth of output in 1991–92, as inventory levels were already low. In countries like India, where import-to-GDP ratios are low, a 'forced' cut in imports tends to affect output more than proportionately.

After April 1991, the effects of the import compression were further accentuated by a number of other factors. First, the collapse of the rupee trade with the former USSR coupled with the recession in Western countries affected the overall demand for exports in traditional markets. Second, the fiscal adjustment and slowdown in government expenditure (which was essential to stabilize the economy) affected the demand for investment goods. Third, the increase in interest rates (which was necessitated by overall monetary considerations) increased the cost of investment and private demand for credit. All these factors, combined with continued import compression, had an adverse effect on output.

An important study by Maurice Scott, published in 1989, after a careful analysis of developments in the US and the UK, came to the conclusion that 'investment' was a much more important proximate cause of growth than what conventional theory (backed up by many growth-accounting studies) had highlighted.[1] The large body of empirical growth-accounting studies showed that changes in capital stock and changes in employment often accounted for only about half of the output growth, the remainder being generally attributed to 'technical progress'. According to these studies, it was the increase in 'total factor productivity' that was more important in determining the rate of growth of industrial output. Scott, however, argued that this result depended crucially on defining capital and investment too narrowly—in terms of 'net' investment rather than 'gross' investment—and that if a correction was made for this factor, the rate of investment emerged as the most crucial variable for accelerating industrial growth. According to Scott, in addition to the direct effects of investment on growth, there were also substantial large positive 'external' and 'learning' effects of investment, whereby investment by one firm created investment opportunities for other firms.

The data for nineteen developing countries, which achieved rates of growth of 6 per cent per annum over the twenty-five-year period 1965–90, also showed that all of them, with a couple of exceptions, had a high rate of growth of investment and a high level of investment during the entire period. In India's case, too, there is some evidence that periods of high industrial growth were also periods of high growth in capital formation in manufacturing. After Independence, there were three periods when India achieved rates of growth of about 8 per cent per annum in industrial and manufacturing production. These periods were 1954–55 to 1965–66, 1975–76 to 1978–79 and 1984–85 to 1990–91. All these years also witnessed a substantially higher rate of growth of capital formation in manufacturing. We cannot be sure about the 'causal link' between the two, or about which came first, growth or investment. However, the association between the two is too strong to be ignored. It is most likely that investment and growth reinforce each other; higher investment causes high growth, which in turn provides incentives for further investment.

One should not, of course, exaggerate the importance of increasing the 'quantity' of investment vis-à-vis the 'efficiency' of investment. Efficiency and the quality of investment are equally important, and a rise in the capital-to-output ratio (or a reduction in efficiency) can easily offset the gains from higher investment. This has happened in India in the case of several large projects. The former USSR is an even better example of the waste of capital; as an expert observer pointed out, 'No society more driven by the demands of investment than that of the Soviet Union could have used investment to so little effect.'[2] It is certainly possible to combine high investment with low growth. However, the converse is not true—there are very few cases of high industrial growth preceded by low investment. It stands to reason that, without new investment in capital equipment and efficiency-enhancing technologies, industrial growth cannot be sustained for very long.

In looking for a strategy for higher industrial growth, let us, therefore, try and identify those factors that facilitate higher investment by industry in new plants and technology. Some of these crucial factors, based on the global experience so far, are highlighted below.

(A) Macroeconomic Stability

There is abundant evidence from past experience in India and other countries that macroeconomic stability is a necessary (though not sufficient) condition for growth in industrial investment. Long-term confidence in the economy is weakened by instability, and investment is discouraged and made more inefficient. The desire to make quick gains from arbitrage and speculative activities overcomes the desire to make long-term investments in commodity-producing sectors. Instability can be the result of mistakes in macroeconomic policies for political or other reasons, or it may result from events over which the government has no control.

Between 1988 and 1991, both sources of macroeconomic instability were present in India. It witnessed two general elections, three changes of government, several destabilizing domestic developments, the Gulf War (which imposed an extraordinary burden on the economy) and the collapse of the Soviet Union. The resulting macroeconomic instability, apart from causing direct financing and fiscal problems, inevitably affected the environment for long-term investments. The restoration of macroeconomic stability is, therefore, crucial for investment and growth. It is also an important objective of the stabilization programme launched by the government. If India succeeds in stabilizing the economy, despite some short-term costs, the medium- and long-term outlook for investment and employment will definitely improve.

(B) The 'Demand' Situation

We must recognize that there may be a conflict between policies for stabilization and policies for boosting investment. Tight monetary and fiscal policies are good for stabilization, but they increase the costs and risks associated with investments. A situation of high profits and strong demand fosters growth, while low profits and weak demand are necessary to keep inflation in check. During the recent period, even though the growth of money supply in the economy was high—close to 20 per cent in 1991—a number of industries were still facing demand problems. This could be due to a reduction in government expenditure, an important source of demand for many industries. It could also be due to greater flow of funds into financial markets as well as due to the postponement of discretionary consumer expenditure by fixed-income groups in view of the price rise. The collapse of the Soviet trade and the recessionary conditions in the countries in the Organization for Economic Cooperation and Development

(OECD) also affected the demand situation for industries dependent on markets. Whatever the proximate causes of a perceived slackness in demand, it is clear that low profits and low demand are not good for investment.

What can be done, assuming that tight monetary and fiscal conditions are necessary for some more time, to stabilize the economy? In such a situation, it is unrealistic to expect any significant increase in public investment. The best strategy for industrial firms under the circumstances would be to concentrate investment in areas not as closely dependent on the current domestic-demand situation.

One obvious area is exports. The outlook for exports has never been more promising than it is now. The export-profitability picture has improved substantially, while policy hurdles in production and investment have been more or less eliminated, with many firms having acquired a foothold (or at least a 'toehold') in foreign markets. Another potential advantage for India is that wage costs are rising much faster in several East Asian countries that had exhibited dramatic export performance in the 1970s and 1980s. India's share in world trade is less than 0.5 per cent, which means that an expansion in its exports from new investments need not necessarily depend on an expansion of overall demand in the world economy. Our problems are the lack of exportable products of acceptable quality. This is the right time to invest in new products and new technologies for exports.

Much of Indian industry suffers from obsolescence. In a more competitive environment in the future, only those firms are likely to survive that are constantly upgrading their technologies and their output mix. With the virtual abolition of licensing, new firms are likely to enter all profitable lines of manufacturing. These firms will have the advantage of having access to modern technologies and new products to meet old demands. At the same time, existing firms have the advantage of location, cheaper real estate, a trained workforce and an existing marketing network. These initial advantages can become immensely valuable if new investments are made to replace old technologies and machines.

Another important area where there is immense potential for further investment, even under conditions of low final demand, is that of 'energy efficiency'. Indian industry is, by and large, an inefficient user of energy, as its energy use per unit of output is substantially higher than that in other countries. It is reasonable to assume that, with changes in our energy-pricing policy and the exchange-rate regime, the cost of energy in India, over a period of time, will increase at a rate that is higher than the price of the manufactured products. It follows that investment in energy efficiency, even under conditions of tight overall demand, can be an important source of higher profitability for industry.

These are some opportunities for investment not dependant on the state of current domestic demand. There are, no doubt, many more such areas. If a large number of units start investing in these and other areas, this will soon become a self-reinforcing process, with higher investment generating higher growth, higher demand and even higher investment.

(C) Finance

A well-functioning financial system is essential for the growth of investment. There are two aspects of the financing problem: availability and cost. So far as availability is concerned, more savings are likely to be available for private investment in the future than has been the case in the recent past. The government is committed to reducing its fiscal deficit, which simply means that its borrowings from banks and households are going to decline as a percentage of the country's GDP. Thus, domestic savings, which would have otherwise gone into government consumption or public investment, would be available for private investment. This is a crucial point. If the government borrows less, there is more money available for investment elsewhere. For this to happen, however, it is necessary to ensure that a reduction in government borrowings does not lead to a fall in incomes and aggregate savings. This further underlines the need to create a favourable environment for investment, as growth and savings in the economy can be maintained only if investment grows. Otherwise, both savings and incomes will settle at a lower level.

There has been an increase in the cost of capital in the past few years, and the long-term real rates of interest, i.e., the nominal rates *minus* inflation in the economy are about 6–7 per cent. These rates are higher than those prevailing in industrialized as well as in some semi-industrialized countries. In view of the scarcity of capital in India, one would expect real-interest rates to be higher than those prevailing in capital-surplus countries, and most economists would probably agree that from a long-run point of view, there is a case for real-interest rates to be lower than they are. There are, however, two problems in achieving this objective. First, India continues to have a highly complex structure of interest rates (despite recent improvements), with several highly concessional rates. As a result, normal or non-concessional interest rates tend to be higher than they have to be. Second, the growth of money supply has been higher than targeted in recent years.

Interest-rate policy, therefore, has to respond to the need for restraining money supply.

It is to be hoped that the macroeconomic situation will stabilize sufficiently soon to permit further rationalization of the interest rate structure. There is, however, one change that can be introduced in interest-rate policy without affecting the current stance of monetary and credit policy. During a period when interest rates are high for contra-cyclical reasons, there is a tendency on the part of entrepreneurs to postpone investment decisions to avoid 'locking-in' at the prevailing high interest rates. Most countries have, therefore, introduced a system of variable interest rates, whereby interest rates on long-term instruments vary every six months or so in line with movements in the market interest rates and the overall macroeconomic situation. A similar system of variable interest rates should be introduced in India for long-term funds so there is no incentive to postpone investments in anticipation of a fall in rates. A system of variable interest rates is also likely to be favourable for banks and financial institutions.

(D) Fiscal Policy

The role of fiscal policy in promoting investments in general, or in special regions, has long been debated by fiscal experts. A number of countries, including India, have experimented with various types of investment allowances or deposit schemes. While no conclusive evidence on the efficacy of these schemes in promoting aggregate investment is yet available, by and large, the present consensus among fiscal experts is in favour of moderate corporate rates of taxation without special incentives against a system of high rates combined with special deductions for investments in new plants or particular regions. The former system is expected to be less distortional and avoids the possibility of the wasteful use of resources in low-yielding and inefficient activity merely to take advantage of fiscal privileges. There is, however, a strong case for depreciation provisions to be generous, particularly if the rate of inflation is relatively high. The replacement of capital has to take place at current prices, while depreciation is at the book value. During periods of relatively high inflation, liberal depreciation provisions are required to avoid taxation of 'illusory' profits.

Another investment-related issue in the area of fiscal policy is the taxation of capital-goods imports. Here, too, there is a conflict as we have a well-established capital goods industry, which, because of various factors, needs tariff protection. At the same time, in order to reduce costs and make user industries more competitive, it is necessary to reduce import duties to more reasonable levels. Some balance has to be struck, and the government has already announced its intention to reduce import duties over a period of time. The phased reduction is expected to provide lead time for the domestic industry to modernize itself and become more cost-competitive.

(E) Import Policy and Foreign Collaborations

Policies relating to imports, foreign collaborations and foreign investments have already been considerably liberalized, and now there seems to be an extremely attractive environment for new investments. Problems that persist should be sorted out easily, as the government's overall approach is very clear: both import and foreign investment policy are supportive of domestic investments.

(F) Infrastructure

Policies for private investment in the infrastructure and
power sectors have also been liberalized, and these should
provide an additional avenue for higher aggregate investment.
However, in the foreseeable future, the primary responsibility
for providing infrastructure facilities and power remains with
the government, both Central and state. In the changed
environment, where the government is reducing its role
in licensing and controlling economic activities, the most
important contribution of state governments would be to
improve the operational efficiency of infrastructure and power
plants under their command. The old secretariat-oriented
management style will not work, and a new management
structure for state public-sector infrastructure industries must
be created as soon as possible.

(G) An 'Efficient' Public Sector

According to Dandekar, in 1988–89, as much as 53 per cent
of the GDP in mining, manufacturing, construction, power
and finance originated in the public sector.[3] In 1960–61, the
contribution of the public sector to the GDP in these areas
was only 11 per cent; in 1980–81, it was about 40 per cent.

With a contribution of more than half the GDP in
manufacturing, mining, construction, power and finance
(taken together), it is obvious that the future of the economy
will be closely linked, for some time, to the performance of
enterprises in these sectors. It is not a question of profitability
alone but also of their contribution production and growth
of investment in the economy. The government is no longer
in a position to subsidize their operational losses or to provide

adequate resources for further investment. In this situation, their survival and growth are likely to increasingly depend on their own performance. However, it is important to remember that what happens to public-sector enterprises cannot be a matter of indifference to the rest of the economy. These enterprises are closely linked to other enterprises and other sectors as suppliers and as buyers of goods and services. If the public sector fails to function, the rest of the economy will fail as well, at least over the next five to ten years.

The privatization of ownership and the management of selected public enterprises provides a possible answer, but in the Indian situation, it can only provide a partial answer. Partial disinvestment of equity is feasible and desirable to raise resources, but, otherwise, the public sector is too large to be capable of being fully privatized in the near future. Apart from the intricate operational and financial issues (such as valuation), a number of complex issues, particularly in relation to labour, would have to be sorted out. In most market economics, including the UK and Malaysia, successful privatization has been a slow process. The privatization of ownership and management should begin with smaller enterprises in the service, consumer and other simpler manufacturing industries; it can then be extended to other industries, depending on the experience. Meanwhile, answers have to be found to the problems posed by public enterprises, so they do not drag down the rest of the economy.

To conclude, with an appropriate policy framework, India should be able to achieve a rate of industrial growth of 8 to 9 per cent per annum in the long run. This order of growth was realized from time to time in the previous decades despite various problems and several domestic and external setbacks. In the 1980s, a growth rate of this magnitude was achieved in eight out of ten years. In the 1990s and beyond India did even better. The key to higher industrial growth is efficient investment, and this is where the government should concentrate in the future.

4

Finance and Development:
A Shifting Paradigm[*]

In early development economics, during the Planning era, the role of the financial system in the process of capital accumulation was relatively limited. All allocation decisions were expected to be made by the central planning authorities and not by the financial markets. To a large extent, the financial system also had a limited role in providing incentives for savings and capital accumulation, as interest rates were controlled and generally 'repressed', and household savings were pre-empted through high levels of statutory reserve and liquidity ratio.

The above development paradigm shifted rather sharply in the 1990s. Almost all the developing countries adopted a more market-determined strategy of development. There were

---

[*] Based on the Annual Foundation Lecture at the Administrative Staff College of India, Hyderabad, December 1999.

several factors that contributed to this change in perception. The first and foremost reason for questioning the earlier strategy was the simple fact that the actual results in terms of growth of incomes or industrial development were well below expectations. Despite substantial increase in the domestic saving rates in several countries, including India, the rate of growth of incomes was relatively low. The period of relatively low growth also coincided with a period of virtually persistent and recurring balance-of-payments crises.

The change in the development paradigm also led to a change in the perception about the role of the financial system in development. It became clear that the liberalization of product markets also required a well-functioning financial system for the mobilization and allocation of savings. Banks, capital markets and financial institutions were no longer seen as mere conduits for channelling savings in predetermined directions but as important instruments for allocating savings among alternative investment choices according to their relative efficiency.

After the onset of the East Asian crisis in mid-1997, there was a further change in the perception about the role of the financial system in development. Earlier, the real economy was supposed to lead and shape the financial system. During the East Asian crisis, this perception changed dramatically. It became clear that it was the weak financial system that led to the collapse of the real economy. As such, proper development of the financial system was no longer regarded as an 'ancillary' or as adjunct to the development of the real sector, but as a necessary precondition for growth.

The above developments in the real world were supported by findings in theoretical literature, which demonstrated the critical role of the financial system in the growth process. The financial liberalization literature developed in 1970s and 1980s stressed the costs of 'financial repression', particularly interest-rate and exchange-rate controls that restricted the growth of financial intermediation and the real rate of economic growth. These findings were buttressed by the emergence of endogenous growth literature, which emphasized the importance of the financial market as a source of innovation and productivity growth. It was demonstrated that an efficient and well-functioning financial system contributed to economic growth by raising the level of saving and investment and the productivity of capital.

Over time, it was also recognized that financial markets indeed had certain special characteristics. The most important of these was the large volume of transactions and the speed with which financial resources could move from one market and one instrument to another. A related characteristic was the scope for instant 'arbitrage', as between different markets and between different types of instruments. Financial transactions were highly leveraged, and the risk of failure was transferred by the actual decision-makers to innocent bystanders.

Another interesting characteristic of financial markets was the role of financial intermediaries. There were segments of financial markets, such as stock markets and bond markets, where savers themselves made the decision about when and where their money should be used. Markets were, however, also dominated by financial intermediaries (such as banks, provident funds, pension funds and mutual funds), which took investment decisions as well as risks on behalf of their depositors. Yet another important emerging characteristic of financial markets was the so-called 'negative' externalities associated with them. A failure in any one segment of these markets could affect all other segments of the market, including the non-financial markets.

Financial markets also became highly susceptible to 'self-fulfilling' prophecies or expectations. Sometimes 'self-fulfilling' expectations could lead to panic, as the behaviour of a limited group of operators was generalized. Jagdish Bhagwati has described the classic case of a self-fulfilling prophecy with reference to the behaviour of exchange rates dating back to the 1960s. Here is an excerpt from an article written by him, in which he illustrates this particular feature of the foreign-exchange market:

> Let the objective reality initially be that the dollar will not depreciate. But suppose that speculators expect the opposite, and move out of the dollar, depreciating it. If the reality were independent of the actions of the speculators, the dollar would go up again, and the market would have chastised and ruined the speculators. But it may well be that as the dollar falls initially with the speculation and wages, and hence prices, rise in sympathy. If so, the objective reality would itself have changed, legitimating the devaluation of the dollar in view of the speculation-induced rise of prices. Such self-justifying speculation shapes its own reality.[1]

In view of the externalities, volatility and certain other special characteristics, it was generally agreed that financial markets had to be closely monitored and supervised. It also became evident that, in view of the growing integration of worldwide financial markets, failure and vulnerability in the domestic market in a particular country could have international implications. Similarly, problems in the external markets could create difficult problems for the functioning of the domestic markets, even if the country concerned was following prudent macroeconomic policies. This close relationship between the two markets, domestic and external, raised the question of appropriate duties and responsibilities of domestic supervisory authorities and international financial institutions.

Most of these issues came to the fore in the context of the East Asian crisis and subsequent developments in certain other countries such as Russia and Brazil. Let us briefly look at the issues arising from the recent developments in East Asia and elsewhere in the 1990s.

Lessons from the Asian Crisis

Much has been said and written about the causes of the Asian crisis and its aftermath. The literature is voluminous and, in some ways, it is as impressive as the earlier literature on the 'Asian miracle' and raises the obvious question of what developing countries must learn from their successes. It is not proposed to review this literature, nor to comment on what went wrong and what policies could have been handled better either before or after the crisis. The purpose here is limited and confined to recapturing some aspects of the Asian crisis that may have a bearing on our understanding of the relationship between finance and development, and the lessons that countries like India need to keep in view to avoid having to go through similar devastating experiences in the future.

An important point to remember in this connection is that even relatively small mistakes in the conduct of macroeconomic or exchange-rate policies can sometimes lead to big crises. The Asian experience is certainly mixed, and the magnitude of macroeconomic and other policy failures in different East Asian countries was not the same. However, in several of them, the degree of deviation from the best practices or prudent policies was relatively small. It may be that they persisted with the defence of the pegged exchange rates for a week or two longer than was desirable, or it may be that they did not take corrective monetary or fiscal action early enough. However, the devastation and the pain that their economies went through because of these policy mistakes were sizeable and unprecedented.[2]

Incidentally, this was also the experience of Mexico and Argentina in early 1995, when a major emerging crisis was brought under a semblance of control by a massive international rescue effort launched by the IMF, the United States and the World Bank. It is no coincidence that in all these cases, in East Asia as well as in Mexico and Argentina, the proximate cause was the relatively sudden reversal of capital flows, on which these economies had become excessively dependent. It had taken a relatively long time to build a climate of confidence and for capital inflows to rise gradually. However, it took no time for this confidence to dissipate and foreign capital to disappear. It is also interesting to note that the major reversal was not only on account of foreign lenders or investors but also on account of resident holders of domestic assets who rushed to encash or convert their holdings into foreign currency.

The point is, simply, that handling capital flows is not an easy matter. While capital account liberalization and large capital movements have brought considerable growth benefits, they have also brought with them greater potential for volatility in asset prices and financial markets, including forex markets. This can cause unanticipated damage to the real economy during periods of uncertainty about the future economic or political outlook. As mentioned earlier, adverse expectations about a country's future during periods of uncertainty can often become 'self-fulfilling'. The fact that such volatility can be aggravated by a weak financial system, leading to severe development problems, also requires to be borne in mind. The lesson from the Mexican or East Asian episodes is not an argument against capital flows or capital account convertibility. It is about the careful and judicious handling of such flows and about the pace of movement towards capital account liberalization for residents. It is also about building domestic safety nets, for example, by keeping the level of liquid foreign-exchange reserves high in relation to short-term external obligations.

It cannot be denied that, despite the earlier spectacular successes, the financial systems of East Asian countries were characterized by several weaknesses. Thus, banks were not subject to effective prudential regulation and supervision. Credit expansion in these countries was large and banks took untenable positions in real estate and other unproductive assets, building up, in the process, large asset-liability and currency mismatches. Banks had also built up huge off-balance-sheet liabilities, which moved on to the balance sheet once there was adversity. Cross-border inter-bank positions were also large. Non-banking financial companies contributed to the crisis as these were subject to little or no regulation.

Corporates were also highly leveraged. External debt was available at low interest rates, and the fixed exchange rates in these countries offered them a false sense of complacency, encouraging them to hold large unhedged positions. External debt was high, short-term, leveraged and concentrated in the private sector. Thus, on the whole, there was an inherent vulnerability in the financial sector, and once expectation turned adverse, this vulnerability translated itself into a panic. Standards of accounting practices, financial reporting and disclosure norms were somewhat inadequate in these countries. There was a lack of transparency in the operations of market participants as well as in the central banks, in some cases.

Events in East Asia have certainly highlighted the two-way interaction between the financial sector and development and the need for an appropriate policy framework. Improving the efficiency of the financial sector through market-based reforms is an important concern of the new development paradigm. However, this has to be accompanied by policies, practices and a certain amount of restraints that strengthen the financial system towards stability so that growth becomes sustainable. At the same time, proper emphasis has to be placed on growth policies that do not give rise to problems resulting in systemic instability in the financial sector (for example, a large fiscal deficit).

A related issue is that of striking an appropriate balance between financial regulation and market freedom. While freedom is essential to foster efficiency, it also raises an equally important question of an appropriate regulatory framework, given the wide divergence between private and social interest in ensuring the stability of financial system. Hence, a proper system of regulation relating to prudent risk limits, short-term foreign borrowing and the degree of tolerable maturity mismatches in the banking system assumes critical importance for minimizing risks to the stability of the financial system.

The most important lesson emerging from the Asian crisis is the need to be vigilant about domestic and international developments that may impinge on a country's financial relations with the rest of the world. The process of integration of worldwide financial markets has resulted in product innovation and efficiency, but it has also made developing countries subject to greater vulnerability and new risks. Strong fundamentals alone cannot provide full immunity from a crisis. There is a need to take early preventive action, to build firewalls and to keep some safety nets handy.

The Indian Experience

Against the backdrop of the lessons from the Asian crisis, it will be useful to examine issues relating to India from the perspective of our past experience, the present stage of development and policy framework for the future.

As is well known, India's development strategy for nearly forty years or so after Independence placed emphasis on state-guided development initiatives, with the primary role assigned to the state and its agencies for the mobilization and allocation of savings. It was not until the Eighth Plan that the role of the financial sector and financial markets was given an explicit recognition in the development strategy. The emphasis on accelerating investment rate through state intervention in a number of key areas meant channelling credit to certain preferential sectors at subsidized interest rates, exercising public ownership control on banks and restricting their activities through policy prescriptions. Some of the typical features that got built into this system were the directed lending programme with high levels of cash reserve ratio and statutory liquidity ratio, the ceiling on deposit and lending rate, lending to priority sectors, branch licensing and the detailed regulation of banks' loan and investment portfolios.

As far as external finance is concerned, India relied primarily on bilateral and multilateral official development assistance and did not encourage private external capital inflows as a way to supplement domestic savings. The exchange rate was administered, and there was extensive control over all foreign-exchange transactions, which were subject to approval on a case-by-case basis. Because of pervasive exchange controls, the Indian financial system remained largely insulated from international markets. This, however, did not prevent India from suffering regular balance-of-payments crises year after year and becoming dependent on aid flows or credits from the IMF.

The financial system, as a result, faced little or no competition, either domestic or foreign, and costs and efficiency of transactions were not its primary concern. Productivity was generally poor and profitability low. The system was also subject to limited accountability. By the beginning of the 1990s, it was becoming evident that the system could not be sustained without a thorough revamping of its operations.

The balance-of-payments crisis in 1990–91 proved to be the trigger point of reform in several sectors, including the financial sector. The reform initiatives in the financial sector started with the government appointing two committees: one on balance of payments under the chairmanship of Dr C. Rangarajan, which went into the liberalization of policies in the external sector; and the second on the financial sector, under the chairmanship of M. Narasimham, which deliberated on domestic financial-sector reforms. The reforms programme in the financial sector after 1992 largely followed the broad approach set out by these two committees, supplemented by the Second Narasimham Committee, which was set up in 1997.

Financial Reforms in the 1990s

In so far as the 'arithmeticals' of reform in the financial sector—to use a phrase used by the Narasimham Committee—are concerned, significant progress was made in 1990s. There was a steady decline in the level of resource pre-emption from the banking system. Both cash reserve ratio and statutory liquidity ratio were reduced from their high levels of 15 per cent and 38.5 per cent, respectively, to 9 per cent and 25 per cent in 1991–92. Interest rates in various segments of financial markets were deregulated in a phased manner. This preceded the abolition of controls on capital issues and the freeing of the interest rate on private bonds and debentures. While the government borrowing rates were market-determined, there was a gradual phasing out of interest rate subsidies on bank loans. Wide-ranging reforms were initiated to develop and deepen the government securities market, money market, capital market and foreign-exchange market. The so-called 'bank rate' was reactivated, and regular short-term repos (repurchase agreements) were being conducted at a pre-announced rate, and a system of prime lending rate was introduced to provide direction to the movement of interest rates in the credit market.

In the sphere of external financial policy, while the exchange rate was market-determined, over the years, there was a progressive liberalization of foreign direct and portfolio investment, and approval procedures were considerably simplified. As a result, restrictions on inflow of capital into the economy were significantly reduced. There was also a significant liberalization of policy regarding industry's access to foreign equity and borrowing through long-term debt instruments. The banking sector was given a greater degree of freedom with regard to raising funds abroad and managing their external liability, subject to prudential guidelines. The end result of all these and other reforms was the growing integration among the various segments of financial markets, closer convergence of the Indian financial system with the practices prevailing in international financial markets, and greater opportunity for investors to access both domestic and international markets.

Competitive conditions in the banking industry were facilitated by relaxing entry and exit norms and permitting public-sector banks to raise additional capital from the market (up to a certain level). While public-sector banks continued to be predominant, the changing competitive environment in the banking sector made a substantial difference in banking practices and disclosure requirements.

Prudential regulation and supervision also formed a critical component of the financial sector reform programme. India adopted international prudential norms and practices with regard to capital adequacy, income recognition, provisioning requirement and supervision. These norms were progressively tightened over the years, particularly against the backdrop of the Asian crisis. The required capital adequacy ratio was increased to 9 per cent from 8 per cent in the banking sector. The mark-to-market practice for valuation of government securities was also gradually enhanced from 30 per cent in 1992–93 to 75 per cent by 1999–2000. As a further prudential measure against credit and market risks, risk weights were made applicable to government and other securities to take account of price variations.

An attempt was also made to avoid the problems arising from 'connected lending'. The exposure of individual banks and non-banking finance companies to any particular borrower or groups of borrowers were prescribed, and the banking system's exposure to real estate was also limited. Prudent limits were placed on the financial system and the corporate sector on foreign borrowings.

In the area of supervision, a full-fledged institutional mechanism was developed, keeping in view the needs of a strong and stable financial system. The system of off-site surveillance was combined with periodical on-site supervision for monitoring the risk profile of banks and their compliance with prudential guidelines. The Basel Core Principles for Effective Banking Supervision were adopted, and a rating system for Indian banks was also introduced. The Reserve Bank of India's regulatory and supervisory responsibility was widened to include financial institutions and non-banking financial companies.

As a result of these and other measures, some progress in the performance of the Indian banking system was noticeable. The trend in the erosion of profit and capital base was reversed. The net profits of the public-sector banks, as a percentage of their total assets, averaged 0.4 per cent during 1994–95 to 1998–99, against the loss of about 1.0 per cent in 1992–93 and 1993–94. The gross non-performing assets (NPAs) of public-sector banks (without allowing for provisions), as a percentage of the total assets, saw a decline. Most of the public-sector banks achieved the prescribed capital-adequacy ratios. The improved performance also enabled most of the banks to meet their capital requirements from internal resources and the market, without excessive dependence on budgetary support.

The consolidation of the financial system, during the second half of the 1990s, increased the resilience of the Indian economy to external crisis. This was evident from the muted impact of the Asian crisis on the Indian financial markets. Since then, there has been a constant effort to enhance the regulatory and supervisory standards in conformity with international standards.

To sum up, there was considerable progress in the broadening and strengthening of India's financial system in the last decade of the twentieth century. Let us briefly look at some of the areas that require consideration in the future.

Agenda for the Future

The agenda for the future is long. Fortunately, there has been a widespread interest and debate among experts and market participants on the various aspects of financial reform that enabled India to chart out a path best suited for it. A few areas that deserve our attention, on priority, in the future are mentioned below.[3]

First and foremost, it is necessary to continue with the process of strengthening India's prudential, provisioning and capitalization norms and bring them in line with the best international standards. It is equally important to continue with efforts to introduce maximum transparency, disclosure and accountability, so that the investors and counterparties to financial transactions can make their decisions based on full and complete information and their own assessment of market (and other) risks. Tighter and tougher prudential standards will, no doubt, cause some pain and impose greater responsibility on banks and other financial institutions. However, given the new international focus, and externalities and linkages involved, the regulation of the financial sector is no longer a matter of choice or a matter of domestic concern alone. Over a period of time, it is likely that the willingness of the rest of the world to do financial business—by way of trade credits, direct investments or other types of investments and loans—will depend on their confidence in India's financial practices. India must remain ahead of the curve in its prudential management.

The level of NPAs of the banking system in India had shown some improvement in the 1990s, but it was still too high. A part of the problem in resolving this issue was the carry-over of old NPAs in certain declining sectors of industry. The problem was further complicated by the fact that there were a few banks that were fundamentally weak, and their potential to return to profitability, without substantial restructuring, was low. The Narasimham Committee and the Verma Committee looked into the problems of weak banks and made certain recommendations that were considered by government and the Reserve Bank. These were also widely debated so that an acceptable long-term solution could be evolved. Leaving aside the problem of weak banks, in profitable banks, too, the NPA levels were found to be relatively high. In the future, vigorous effort has to be made by these banks to strengthen their internal control and risk-management systems, and to set up early warning signals for timely detection and action. The resolution of the NPA problem also requires greater accountability on the part of corporates, greater disclosures in the case of defaults and an efficient credit information system. With the help of stricter accounting and prudential standards, the problem of NPAs in the future could be effectively contained.

In order to allow for growth in their assets in line with real growth in the economy, banks and financial institutions would also need to increase their capitalization quite substantially over time. The minimum shareholding by the Reserve Bank in the State Bank of India (SBI), prescribed by legislation in the 1990s, was 55 per cent. The minimum percentage of shareholding by the government in public-sector banks was 51 per cent. A number of strong banks were able to access capital markets to meet their capitalization requirements in line with prudential guidelines. However, some of these banks, including the SBI, had limited scope with regard to raising further capital from the market within the prescribed floor of the Reserve Bank and government shareholdings. If the risk-weighted assets of these banks grow in line with the growth in the economy in the early twenty-first century, the additional capital requirements of these banks could exceed Rs 10,000 crore. Against this requirement, the headroom available for these banks to raise capital from the market at the end of 1990s was less than Rs 1000 crore. After allowing for additional infusion of reserve capital through internal generation and access to subordinated debt, the gap between their additional capital requirement and the leeway available to raise capital from the market will remain quite sizeable for several years.

In this situation, an issue that needs to be debated and resolved is whether this gap should be filled by contribution from the Reserve Bank (in the case of SBI) and the government (in the case of other public-sector banks), or whether the legislative ceiling for capital to be subscribed by the public should be raised. The provision of additional capital by the Reserve Bank is tantamount to additional monetization, and its monetary impact is equivalent to that of printing additional currency. Contribution to banks' capital by the government has a similar effect as it will add to the government's deficit, which is already high. The government, in any case, would need to provide additional capital to weak banks, which are not in a position to raise capital on their own. Does it make economic or fiscal sense to add to this burden further? On balance, there seems to be a strong case for raising the legislative ceiling for market participation in the equity capital of public-sector banks.

At the same time, it has to be recognized that, in view of the need to give adequate attention to agricultural credit and rural banking as also to maintain public confidence in the safety of banks, the public-sector character of these banks should not be given up. Keeping these considerations in view, i.e., allowing greater access to markets while at the same time maintaining the public-sector character of banks owned by the government or the Reserve Bank, it would be necessary to prescribe a maximum (at a suitably low level) for shareholding by any single individual or a corporate in public-sector banks. The government should also retain the pre-emptive right to appoint, if it wishes, the chief executive and the majority of the board members in public-sector banks.

Over the years, the progressive liberalization of financial markets and institutional reforms have led to growing interlinkages among the various segments of financial markets. The emergence of different types of financial intermediaries, in addition to banks and financial institutions, is healthy and desirable. A diversified structure contributes to greater stability of the financial system in the event of unanticipated problems. Part of the reason why problems in Japan's financial sector have persisted for so long is believed to be due to virtually 'bank only' financial intermediation.

In India, while there has been progress in developing the various segments of markets, including the money and debt markets, the depth of these markets remains low, and the volumes as well as number of participants are not very large. An important priority for the future is to develop the depth and breadth of these markets and to allow a multiplicity of intermediation possibilities with different risks and leverage profiles. The Reserve Bank of India should continue to work with financial experts and market participants to develop an appropriate procedural and policy framework to move in this direction.

India also has to devise measures to make the interest-rate structure more flexible in order to take account of changes in economic cycles and the inflation outlook. For reasons highlighted in the Mid-term Review of Monetary and Credit Policy in October 1999, there are several constraints that limit the flexibility of interest rates in the banking sector and the rest of the financial sector. Given the fact that some of these constraints are deeply embedded in historical practices, consumer preference and public-sector requirements, it may take some time to fully meet this objective. However, the process should begin.

The above are just a few priority areas that require consideration. The list is by no means exhaustive. If India gets this right, it would make movement in other areas of financial reform speedier and easier.

Conclusion

As mentioned earlier, the change in the development paradigm from a largely state-directed strategy to a market-oriented one, and the unsatisfactory results of the earlier strategy, highlighted the role of the financial system in the efficient mobilization and allocation of a society's savings. All over the developing world, in the 1990s, there was intense activity in reviewing the structure of the financial markets and taking measures to liberalize and broaden them.

Against this background, and against the background of past dissatisfactions with the old strategy, it is interesting to note that the record of development in the 1990s was a highly disappointing one for the developing world as a whole, with two important exceptions—India and China. The 1990s—the period of the triumph of capitalism and financial liberalization—saw a growth rate of only 3.2 per cent in world output, which is lower than the average of 3.9 per cent in the 1970s, and not much different from the rate of growth of 3.4 per cent in the 1980s.

The reason for drawing attention to this rather disheartening record in the 1990s is not that India should return to the old, failed strategy in the future; nor is it to suggest that financial liberalization or development of the financial markets is unnecessary. The old strategy collapsed under the weight of its own excesses and contradictions. Similarly, there is no doubt that financial reform and the liberalization of markets is necessary, essential and desirable to derive the maximum advantage from the comparative advantage of nations, the international movement of capital and the momentous changes that are taking place in technology. The purpose in highlighting some of the problems that emerged in the world economy in the 1990s is to underscore simply one point: that we must not confuse 'means' with 'ends'. Financial reforms and the liberalization of markets are the means to an end, not ends in themselves. The final objective of a successful development strategy remains what it has always been: a sustained and rising income for all the people, and the removal of poverty, deprivation and illiteracy within a reasonable period of time.

Alongside financial reform and the development of markets, the country's attention must also turn to the fiscal empowerment of the state and improvement in public administration. Even more than fifty years after Independence, who can deny that India's public offices (including public-sector institutions) leave a lot to be desired in terms of delivery of services or in the efficient discharge of essential functions? A thorough review of the institutional framework, rules, regulations and accountability of the administrative organs of the state is essential at the beginning of the twenty-first century. The focus should be on what they do for the people, not what they do for themselves. If India's public institutions, including those in the field of education and health, are unable to overcome their inertia, then alternative modalities have to be found for delivering these and other services to the people.

Many of the functions of the state are now left undone or inefficiently executed, because of financial stringency at the Centre as well as the states. The dependence on borrowings to finance even essential expenditure has been increasing year after year, leading to a vulnerable and unsustainable fiscal situation. Without adequate finance, the state cannot fulfil its developmental role or remove the constraints to the country's potential output. Pioneering work has been done by research institutions, as well as by the Central and several state governments, to identify measures that need to be taken to reinvigorate the fiscal system. In the twenty-first century, India must move decisively in this direction without losing time.

With a revitalized fiscal situation and further progress in establishing a forward-looking, strong and stable financial system, the first century of the next millennium can truly be a century of development.

INDIA NOW (2000–15)

5

India's Economy in the Twenty-first Century: A New Beginning or a False Dawn?*

The overall picture of the Indian economy at the beginning of the new millennium can be best described as 'a tale of two cities'.[1] At one level, the economy presented a picture of tranquillity, comfort and stability at a time when several countries were badly affected by external problems or foreign-exchange crises. Inflation was low, interest rates were declining, liquidity was plentiful and foreign-exchange reserves were at their highest level ever. On the other hand, the 'real' economy showed signs of persistent weakness. Thus, the growth rate for 2000–01 was only 4 per cent, with many parts of the industrial sector continuing to show very low or negative growth. New investment activity and credit flow to the industrial sector was also weak. India's public and

---

* Based on the Eighteenth Dr C.D. Deshmukh Memorial Lecture, India International Centre, New Delhi, 15 January 2001.

social services were also reported to be among the worst in the world. Thus, while the monetary and financial conditions seemed very positive, the real economy was subdued with low growth in output, investment and employment.

Instances on both sides—the best and the worst of India—could be multiplied. What was the truth, and where was India headed at the beginning of the twenty-first century? To answer this question, a bit of dispassionate introspection is necessary to determine the reasons behind India's successes and failures. It is also necessary that, while looking ahead to the future, our country prepares itself to abandon or modify strategies that have not worked in the past, and move decisively in the direction that maximizes India's comparative advantage in the near future.

The Post-Independence Development Record

As one reflects on the history of human civilization in the millennium that ended, it is surprising to recall just how recent the story of economic growth is. As Paul Krugman has noted in a recent book, 'economic growth, at least economic growth that raises living standards, is a modern invention. From the dawn of history to the eighteenth century, the world was essentially Malthusian. Improvements in technology and capital investments were always overtaken by population growth; the number of people slowly increased, but their average standards of living did not.'[2] Up to about the end of the nineteenth century, the only countries where per capita incomes were increasing on a sustained basis for any length of time were the Western countries, particularly England, Germany, France and the US. During this entire period, the then so-called underdeveloped or Third World countries continued to be exporters of primary products and importers of industrial products with stagnant and, in some cases, declining per capita incomes. A large number of them were also colonies of the Western powers, and the connection between these two situations—the colonial state and income stagnation—was not missed by their leaders and intellectuals.

The development strategies of the newly independent and developing countries, including India, in the mid-twentieth century were framed against this background. The central and leading role for breaking away from the colonial legacy and for speeding up the process of industrialization was assigned to the state. The need for the government to occupy the commanding heights and to lead from the top received further support from the astounding success of the erstwhile Soviet Union in emerging as a rival centre of political and industrial power within a very short period. India, at that time, played a pioneering role in giving expression to the aspirations of the newly independent Third World countries in the economic field. Thus, in 1956, India's Second Five-Year Plan outlined the goals of development strategy in the following terms:

> The pattern of development and the structure of socio-economic relations should be so planned that they result not only in appreciable increases in national income and employment but also in greater equality in incomes and wealth. Major decisions regarding production, distribution, consumption and investment—and in fact all significant social-economic relationships—must be made by agencies informed by social purpose.

In practice, it meant, that all allocation decisions were to be made by the government or its agencies. The need for raising resources for development was, of course, considered important. However, the primary emphasis was to be on increasing the domestic savings rate by suppressing consumption and high taxation, and appropriating profits through the ownership of commercial enterprises. Accelerated capital accumulation through these means was considered to be the key to development. In a celebrated observation that guided many a planner and policymaker in developing countries, Professor W. Arthur Lewis observed:

> The central problem in the theory of economic development is to understand the process by which a community which was previously saving and investing 4 to 5 per cent of its national income or less, converts itself to an economy where voluntary saving is running at about 12 to 15 per cent of national income and more. This is the central problem because the central fact of economic development is rapid capital accumulation (including knowledge and skills with capital).[3]

While the reasons for adopting a centrally directed strategy of development were understandable against the background of the colonial rule, it soon became clear that the actual results of this strategy were far below expectations. Instead of showing high growth, high public savings and a high degree of self-reliance, India was actually showing one of the lowest rates of growth in the developing world, with rising public deficits and periodic balance-of-payments crises. According to one calculation, in thirty out of thirty-five years, between 1956 and 1991, India had balance-of-payment problems of varying intensity. Looking back, it is hard to believe that for as long as forty years, between 1950 and 1990, India's growth rate averaged less than 4 per cent per annum, while the per capita income growth was less than 2 per cent per annum. This was at a time when the developing world, including sub-Saharan Africa and other least developed countries, showed a growth rate of 5.2 per cent per annum.

However, the most striking failure was not in terms of growth, or even in the precarious situation of the balance of payments. Although the argument is not convincing, it could still be debated by some that the low growth outcome was due to a number of factors beyond India's control, such as the border wars, severe droughts, periodic oil shocks and, finally, the inhospitable global environment! The balance-of-payments difficulties could also—with some imagination—be attributed to the global woes of primary producers, and the struggle of a poor developing country like India to industrialize and become self-reliant in heavy industry (which hitherto was the monopoly of the rich industrialized nations). The most conspicuous failure for which there is no alibi, and the responsibility for which lies squarely and indisputably at our doors, is the erosion in public savings and the inability of the public sector to generate resources for investment or the provision of public services.

It may be recalled that an important assumption in the choice of the post-Independence development strategy was the generation of public savings, which could be used for higher and higher levels of investment. However, this did not happen, and the public sector—instead of being a generator of savings for the community's good—became, over time, a consumer of the community's savings. This reversal in roles had become evident by the early 1970s, and the process reached its culmination by the early 1980s. By then, the government began to borrow, not only to meet its own revenue expenditure but also to finance public-sector deficits and investments. During the period 1960–75, the total public-sector borrowings (including government borrowings) averaged 4.4 per cent of the GDP. This figure increased to 6 per cent of the GDP by 1980–81, to a further 9 per cent by 1989–90.

Thus, the public sector, which was supposed to generate resources for the growth of the rest of the economy, gradually became a net drain on society as a whole. It is interesting to note that the Central government's total internal public debt by 1994–95 was close to Rs 5 lakh crore, and nearly one-third of it was accounted for by assets held in the public sector. The interest payments on public debt amounted to nearly Rs 40,000 crore, which was financed by new net borrowings, and they represented nearly 70 per cent of the Centre's fiscal deficit. In effect, by 1994–95, one-third of the interest payments were on account of the government's past investment in the public sector. In the five years since then, the Centre's internal debt almost doubled to Rs 9.7 lakh crore in 1999–2000. This sharp increase in internal debt was partly accounted for by the need to borrow higher and higher amounts to service the past debt.

A large part of the cherished 'family silver' was thus financed out of borrowings, and kept polished with further borrowings by an impoverished family. In the annals of development history, it is hard to find another example of a perfectly sensible idea—the need for higher public investment for the greater public good—leading to exactly the opposite result, i.e., tragically higher public consumption with diminishing returns for the public!

The 1990s: The Shift in the Development Paradigm

The state-dominated development paradigm shifted rather sharply in the 1990s. Almost all the developing countries moved towards a more market-determined strategy of development. There were several factors that contributed to this change in perception. The first and foremost reason for questioning the earlier strategy, as mentioned before, was the simple fact that actual results in terms of growth of incomes or industrial development were well below expectations. While savings rates were rising, as per the Arthur Lewis model, so were capital-output ratios, due to the inefficiencies in the allocation and use of resources.

An equally important factor contributing to the change in perceptions was the astonishing success of Japan and the East Asian countries in accelerating their rates of growth by relying on a market-oriented pattern of industrialization (tempered with, of course, varying degrees of 'guidance' from the state). Japan's per capita rate of growth of 8 per cent per annum during 1953–73 was unprecedented in the history of economic development. No economy had ever grown at that rate before, and Japan emerged from the ruins of war to become the world's second-largest economy. Similar was the record of industrialization in East Asia, particularly in countries like Hong Kong, Singapore, Taiwan and South Korea. In the 1950s, their per capita incomes or the degree of industrialization was no different from those of the rest of Asia. However, within a period of thirty years, they were able to catch up with the industrialized countries of the West. A final and decisive development leading to the demise of the old strategy was the collapse of the Soviet Union and the acceptance of market-led development strategies by all countries of Eastern Europe.

Beginning in 1991, when India was in the midst of an acute economic crisis, the Government of India also introduced a number of measures to improve the working of the economy. These measures, spread over a number of years, had two broad objectives. One was the reorientation of the economy from a statist, centrally directed and highly controlled economy to what is referred to in the current jargon as a 'market-friendly economy'. A reduction in direct controls and physical planning was expected to improve the efficiency of the economy. It was to be made more 'open' to external trade and external flows through a reduction in trade barriers and the liberalization of foreign-investment policies. A second objective of the reform measures was macroeconomic stabilization. This was to be achieved by substantially reducing fiscal deficits and the government's draft on society's savings.

Compared to the historical trend, the impact of these policies was positive and significant. The growth rate of the economy during 1992–93 to 1999–2000 was close to 6.5 per cent per annum. The balance-of-payments position also improved. Current-account deficits were moderate, while India's external debt (as a percentage of the GDP) and debt-servicing burden actually came down since the early 1990s. There was also evidence of considerable restructuring in the corporate sector, with attention being given to cost-competitiveness and financial viability.

After the initiation of economic liberalization in 1991, there is very little doubt that India's economy—by any standard of measurement—had become stronger and more resilient in 2010 than it had been a decade ago. Looking back, it is, of course, a matter of judgement whether this outcome was due to the reform process, astute short-term economic management, favourable external circumstances or just plain good luck! There is also little doubt that India's 'potential' for growth, combined with external and domestic financial stability, is much stronger at the beginning of the twenty-first century than it was twenty, fifty or a hundred years ago.

India in the New Global Economy

A most remarkable feature of the so-called 'new economy' in the twenty-first century is the role of the services sector (of which the IT [or information technology] sector is a part) in generating growth in income and employment. It may be recalled that the focus of attention in conventional economics, including development economics, was on the production of goods—manufactured products and agricultural commodities. It was, of course, recognized that the services sector (which included transport, communication, trade, banking, construction and public administration, etc.,) was an important source of income and employment in most economies. However, overall, the growth of services was perceived, at best, as a by-product of developments in the primary and secondary sectors and, at worst, as a drag on the prospects for long-term economic growth. Services were believed to be mainly non-tradable activities with slow productivity growth and low employment potential. In developing countries, the conventional view of the growth of the services sector was even worse. It was seen to divert scarce resources away from the production of goods and contribute to the accentuation of income inequalities.

In the twenty-first century, there has been a phenomenal change in the conventional view of services and their role in the economy. The development of certain services is regarded as one of the preconditions of economic growth, not as one of its consequences. The boundary between goods and services is also disappearing, as services of various kinds are delinked from the manufacturing process and become essential elements of the productive structure. Many industrial products are not only manufactured, they are also designed, marketed, advertised, distributed, leased and serviced. A significant and rising part of the value added by manufacturers now consists of services.

The change in the image and role of services has been brought about by unprecedented and unforeseen advances in computer and communication technology. An important aspect of the 'services revolution' is that geography and levels of industrialization are no longer the primary determinants of the location of facilities for the production of services. As a result, the traditional role of developing countries is also changing—from being mere recipients to becoming important providers of long-distance services.

From India's point of view, some of the long-term global developments since the 1990s that provide opportunities for substantial growth are:

- The fastest-growing segment of services is the rapid expansion of knowledge-based services, such as professional and technical services. With regard to these services, India has a tremendous advantage because of a developed structure of technological and educational institutions and lower labour costs.
- Progress in information technology is making it increasingly possible to unbundle the production and consumption of information-intensive service activities.

These activities—research and development, computing, inventory management, quality control, accounting, personnel administration, secretarial, marketing, advertising, distribution and legal services—are performed in all economic sectors.

- Unlike most other prices, the world prices of transport and communications services have fallen dramatically over the years. By 1960, sea-transport costs were less than a third of their 1920 level. The cost of a telephone call fell more than tenfold between 1970 and 2000. Moreover, the cost of communication is also becoming independent of distance; the most dramatic example in this area is, of course, provided by the Internet. India's geographical distance from several important industrial markets (for instance, North America) is no longer an important element in the cost structure of skill-based services.

- Further, India does not necessarily have to be a low-cost producer of certain types of goods (for example, computers or discs) before it can become an efficient supplier of services embodied in them (for instance, software or music). It is possible now to provide value-added services without waiting to 'catch up' in technology for the production of sophisticated equipment or products.

- The decline in the share of manufacturing in the output of rich countries implies a relative decline in their demand for industrial raw materials and fuels. This means that the growth in the exports of developing countries now depends less on natural-resource endowments and more on efficiency in providing services and service-intensive goods.

Another important factor in India's favour is international capital mobility and the integration of the global financial markets. Domestic savings continue to be important for development. However, the scarcity of domestic capital is no longer a binding constraint. The increased mobility of capital has ensured that global resources flow to countries that can show high growth and high returns. It is feasible for India to take advantage of a virtuous circle of higher growth, higher external capital inflows, and higher domestic incomes and savings, which in turn can lead to further growth.

At the same time, it must be recognized that the 'death of distance' and the growing integration of global products, services and financial markets also presents new challenges for the management of the national economy—not only in India but all over the world. The trend towards the integration of markets, particularly financial markets, is by no means an unmixed blessing. Unlike the old days, a heavy price may have to be paid by national economies for somnolence, sloth and non-conformity to generally accepted international norms and standards of macroeconomic management, disclosure, transparency and financial accountability. If a country does not put its financial house in order, fresh investments, trade and technology are likely to pass it by. Faced with this situation, only a few countries, with certain special advantages and resource endowments, may still manage to grow at an acceptable rate. Other countries that need capital and external flows to meet their trade or current-account deficits are likely to find it increasingly difficult to meet their import requirements of essential commodities (such as oil), raw materials and machines.

Another consequence of recent global trends is the greater vulnerability of national economies to developments outside their own borders. In addition to the direct effects (which are most visible in the volatile stock markets), the indirect effects due to 'contagion' can be quite serious. A crisis in any one country or group of countries can be transmitted to other countries—including countries that may not have any strong economic linkages with crisis-affected countries.

The lessons from the recent developments are clear. Advances in IT, the increasing role of services, the integration of financial and capital markets and the diminished role of distance provide tremendous new opportunities for countries like India. At the same time, like other countries, India is also subject to greater vulnerability and new risks. Thus, at the beginning of the new century, the challenge before India is to seize the new opportunities while, at the same time, protecting the economy against unanticipated risks. Insularity or isolation is not the answer, as such an approach will promote neither growth nor stability.

India has to move vigorously to take advantage of expanding opportunities in trade and become a choice location for IT and other industries and services so that growth rates, along with employment, are substantially enhanced. It must also keep some safety nets handy by building a diversified and efficient financial system that would be able to aid and protect the development process at all times—good and bad. Can these objectives be met? This is the real question for the future.

India's Tryst with Destiny

There has been a fair amount of debate in the country on the implications of the new directions in India's economic policy. Most (though not all) commentators seem to agree that efficiency in the use of resources and growth performance of the economy need to be improved. There is also broad agreement that the government's fiscal deficits should be reduced, exports should be increased, and that more should be done for improving the health and education of the poor. There is, however, a substantial difference of views on the instruments that should be used to achieve these objectives, and on whether policy the reforms of the 1990s succeeded in raising the growth rate of the economy in the long run. Concern has also been expressed on certain political and social implications of the new policies, particularly about whether they will make the country more amenable to external pressures and hurt the development of the country's domestic resources. These issues are important, and deserve to be fully considered in the evolution of India's economic policy in the twenty-first century.

On balance, keeping in view the actual economic and non-economic results of the old strategy, the phenomenal changes that have taken place in the world economy and India's present comparative advantage, the present direction of policies to make India more open and more competitive, is certainly worthwhile and deserves to be accelerated. Without a major transformation of economic policies and effort to align them with the contemporary realities of global trade, investment and technology, it is not feasible for India to occupy the high ground and realize its full potential for growth and development.

A decisive move towards more (and deeper) economic reforms is the first strategic priority for the future. However, it will be a grave mistake to misconstrue the need for economic reforms by calling for a lesser role for the government or public policy in widening opportunities and creating a positive environment for equitable development. In developing countries such as India, with massive illiteracy and underdevelopment of infrastructure, the government must continue to play a crucial role in creating the necessary conditions for growth through investments in areas such as education, health, water supply, irrigation, infrastructure, and so on. These tasks cannot be taken over by the market. Successful economic reforms must result in strengthening the ability of governments to do what they need to do by helping to generate higher growth, higher revenue and higher productivity. As the recent experience of several transitional and emerging market economies shows, economic reforms are necessary but by no means a sufficient condition for growth and development.

In this connection, a core issue, with multiple dimensions, which would need to be resolved in the years to come, is what can perhaps be described as a growing 'public–private' dichotomy in India's economy. It is a striking fact that economic renewal and positive growth impulses are now occurring largely outside the public sector—at the level of private corporations (like software companies), autonomous institutions (like the Indian Institutes of Management [IIMs] or the Indian Institutes of Technology [IITs]), or in the case of individuals at the top of their professions in India and abroad. In the governmental or public sector, on the other hand, there is a marked deterioration at all levels—not only in terms of output, profits and public savings but also in the provision of vital public services in the fields of education, health, water and transport. These two elements—fiscal deterioration and the inability to provide essential services— are, of course, intimately connected. Most of India's public resources are currently dissipated in the payment of salaries or for interest on past debt, with little or no resources available for the expansion of public or publicly supported services in vital sectors.

In considering the reasons for the decay and deterioration that is taking place in India's public services, one is reminded of an observation made by A.H. Hanson more than fifty years earlier on the reasons for the then prevailing crisis of Indian planning. He was an admirer of Indian planners, but after seeing the results on the ground, he was compelled to ask:

> The men are able, the organization is adequate, the procedures are intelligently devised. Why, then, have the plans, since 1956, so persistently run into crisis?

Hanson's answer to this question is also revealing:

> For various reasons, Indian planners have never treated the 'objective function' with sufficient respect. Their tendency is to give themselves the fullest benefit of every possible doubt . . . Too many of their aims are contingent upon the adoption, by various sections of the Indian community, of attitudes they are exceedingly unlikely to adopt . . .[4]

That was in 1963! Over time, India's problems in the management of public resources at different levels have only become more and more intractable. Let us look at some of the problems that now bedevil India's public delivery systems:

- The 'authority' of governments, at both the Centre and the states, to enforce their decisions has been eroded over time. Governments can pass orders, for example, for the relocation of unauthorized industrial units or other structures, but implementation can be delayed if they run counter to the private interests of some (at the expense of the general public interest). Similarly, governments may decide to restructure public utilities to cut down waste or output losses, but these decisions do not necessarily have to be implemented if they adversely affect the interests of public servants employed in these organizations.

- Governments at different levels may announce plans and programmes to provide social services (such as expanding literacy), but these initiatives are unlikely to be implemented on the ground because of fiscal stringency. For example, in 1994, the Tenth Finance Commission projected a rate of growth in real terms of 2.5 per cent, for expenditure on elementary education up to the end of the century in respect of four states where the incidence of poverty and illiteracy was among the highest in the country. This projected rate of growth in expenditure was lower than the growth of population in the relevant age group, and grossly insufficient to cover new programmes of adult literates. Since the Tenth Finance Commission's report, it is interesting to note that the real expenditure on elementary education, outside of the salaries of government teachers, in these four states was actually negative!

- The process and procedures for conducting business in government and public service organizations, over time, have become non-functional. There are a multiplicity of departments involved in the simplest of decisions, and administrative rules generally concentrate on the process rather than results. There is very little decentralization of decision-making powers, particularly financial powers. Thus, while local authorities have been given significant authority in some states for implementing national programmes, their financial authority is limited. Transfers to local authorities for health spending, for example, average less than 15 per cent in several state government budgets.

- The multiplicity of functions and responsibilities placed upon ill-equipped and ill-trained staff in public offices and local institutions make it almost impossible to deliver services with any degree of efficiency, particularly in rural areas. For example, a 'multipurpose' female health worker may be required to perform as many as forty-seven tasks to be undertaken on a regular basis!

Let us also consider who suffers the most from fiscal stringency and the atrophy of the public delivery systems. It is certainly not the affluent classes, or persons elected or appointed by the people to serve them. They can always go to private hospitals, private schools, autonomous universities or institutes of higher education, and have similar alternative means of meeting their other requirements. The worst affected are likely to be the poor, the unemployed and the illiterate, who are dependent on public services, public investment and public programmes.

To conclude, there are two important prognostications about India's potential for long-term growth in the twenty-first century that are worth considering. The first is by a well-known Indian economist with a distinguished record of forecasting. He has observed that 'it is possible for India to have a per capita income of US $30,000 by the year 2047. If the Indian economy does as well as some of the world's fast-growing economies have done, it could be even higher.'[5] The second projection is by a professor in business management in the United States.[6] He estimated that, by 2025, India's GDP would exceed that of Japan, and India could then be the third-largest economy in the world (behind the US and China).

Both forecasts, independently arrived at, in two different parts of the world, are, of course, contingent on a number of factors. There is, however, no doubt that if India is able to realize even half its potential in the next twenty or twenty-five years, India's poverty would surely become a distant memory.

6

Politics and Governance

Every ten or fifteen years since Independence, India's reputation has swung from that of a land of great opportunity to that of a country with an uncertain future. At the beginning of the twenty-first century, India's reputation as a democracy and as an emerging global economic power was at its peak. On the other hand, not so long ago, in 1991, India went through one of its worst economic crises. With two short-lived Central governments in two years prior to 1991, there was also a big question mark about the country's political future.

Similarly, in the 1950s, soon after Independence, India was seen as the leader among developing countries, with a strong voice, on their behalf, in international affairs. This position changed dramatically by the mid-1960s, when, after a bad drought, India had to practically beg for food aid from the United States. This difficult period was followed by a triumphant return to power by the Congress government in the 1971 elections in the wake of a clarion call to 'Remove

Poverty' (or 'Garibi Hatao') and support Bangladesh in its struggle for independence. Just four years later, in 1975, a national emergency was declared, followed by a restoration of democracy in 1977, which received worldwide attention. However, the new government, formed by a coalition of parties that were in opposition earlier, did not last long, and in 1979 the country was once again plunged into a deep economic crisis because of political uncertainty, a sharp rise in oil prices and drought.

Taken as a whole, the period from 1966 to 1980 was effectively the darkest period for the Indian economy during the post-Independence period. The annual growth rate was only about 3 per cent, the population growth was higher than 2 per cent per annum (compared with the Plan target of 1.25 per cent), while annual growth in per capita income was less than 1 per cent. The pace of industrialization, which was expected to accelerate with higher investment and higher domestic savings, also plummeted. The rate of growth of industrial production during the period 1965–80 was only 4 per cent per annum, as compared to 7.7 per cent in the earlier fifteen years (1950–65).

Against this dismal historical background, there has been a sea change in India's economic position in the last two decades of the twentieth century and the beginning of the twenty-first century. Despite the economic crisis of 1991, the average annual growth rate since 1981 exceeded 6 per cent, the per capita growth about 4 per cent per annum, while the average life expectancy is estimated to have improved from fifty in 1981 to sixty-five at the turn of the century. India is now regarded as an emerging economic power, and is one of the fastest-growing countries in the world. Only China has grown faster than India over the past twenty-five years. However, in view of recent management problems in public-sector enterprises, particularly in the banking sector, there is increasing scepticism about the ability of the Chinese economy to maintain its growth momentum. India also has one of the highest levels of foreign-exchange reserves in the world in relation to its external debt or share of international trade, and balance-of-payment problems are unlikely to occur again in the foreseeable future. In light of these highly positive developments, it is now commonplace to project India as one of the three most important global economies by 2020 or 2025 (after the United States and China). An annual growth rate of 7.5 to 8 per cent is expected to be within reach in the years ahead. In view of the anticipated decline in population growth, per capita incomes may rise by 6 per cent or more per year. The increase in per capita income of this order would have a substantial impact in reducing poverty and eliminating hunger, malnutrition and illiteracy.

This chapter is an attempt to understand the causes of the swings in India's fortunes from time to time, and explore the reasons for the country's failure to fully realize its potential. Ever since Independence, India has been fortunate for the highly reputed political leaders who did their best to lead the country under difficult circumstances. It has also had the advantage of having a large number of top economists of international stature advise the government in the process of planning and economic policy formulation. In respect of administration, India inherited the so-called 'steel frame' of a permanent bureaucracy from the British era, which was the envy of the postcolonial developing world. And yet, despite all these advantages, over a period of six decades after Independence, economic progress was much slower than anticipated or planned.

Looking at the past record, an unavoidable conclusion is that while economists, political leaders and administrators were working together, on the surface, the reality was vastly different in a more fundamental sense. Despite appearances to the contrary, there was, in fact, a substantial gap between what was considered to be economically sound and what was found to be politically feasible. Economic strategy seldom reflected India's political or social realities or real political considerations. Similarly, the administrative implications of policies, launched with great conviction, were seldom considered or, when considered, these implications did not affect the actual evolution of economic policies or programmes on the ground. For a better future and sustained high growth, it is essential to evolve policies that are practical and pragmatic, and can reconcile the country's economic interests with political realities within a democratic framework.

On the importance of keeping political factors in view while considering economic issues, the observation of Gunnar Myrdal as early as 1957, when development economics and development planning were at an early stage, was highly perceptive. The only certainty, he pointed out, was that 'we shall continuously be surprised by seeing the unexpected happen'. Nothing is permanent, particularly political development.[1]

In considering economic policy issues from a political perspective, as highlighted by I.M.D. Little in 2003, it is also necessary to make a conceptual distinction between the role of the 'State' and that of the 'Government' in power.[2] The state comprises all the legislative, executive and judicial institutions, and the laws governing the inhabitants of the territory to which it lays claim. It also has a monopoly of the use of force over its citizens and over foreigners (as only the state can declare war). Governments, on the other hand, may be thought of as being tenants of the state. They may come and go in accordance with the Constitution or customs of the state. While in office, a government in power—elected or unelected—may change the institutions and laws of the state, but at any given moment it is the agent of the state. While the state is expected to be permanent, the authority of the government to make policy is likely to last as long as it continues to be in office.

This conceptual distinction between the state and the government is vital as it explains why a government—even if freely and duly elected—has to be directly accountable to the people for its actions. The state is the sole and legitimate custodian of public interest and sovereign power, not the government of the day. Public institutions are expected to be permanent (for example, say, the railways, or the universities), and they should not be governed by the whims and fancies of the ministers 'temporarily' in power.

Democracy, Politics and Economics

India's last general elections, held in 2014, when over 550 million voters exercised their right to vote, was the largest democratic election ever held in the world. Indian general elections have also, by and large, been free and fair. All eligible voters, irrespective of caste, creed, religion, income or occupation, have equal rights. An autonomous Election Commission supervises the elections. It has the necessary powers to ensure that the right of voters to vote freely is respected in principle and in practice. The judiciary is vigilant, and its verdict commands the full respect of all concerned, including the party and the government in power. For all

Indians, and others interested in democratic elections, it is an exhilarating feeling to see all candidates, including powerful ministers and the prime minister, campaigning from time to time for the people's votes with the utmost humility and respect.

Since 2014, India has also had the advantage of having a majority government in power for the first time in twenty-five years since 1989. The new government, at the highest level, has also announced a large package of reforms that it wishes to introduce in order to boost investors' confidence and growth. Some important matters that have been proposed to provide benefits to the people include the interstate Goods and Services Tax (GST), insurance and land reforms, the completion of existing public projects (for example, in the power sector or roads), the reduction of the fiscal deficit to budgeted levels and schemes like the Jan-Dhan Yojana. All these proposed economic reforms will certainly contribute to higher growth as and when implemented and will hopefully reduce poverty at an accelerated pace over time. Ultimately, the main task is to implement what has been promised and not wait for long.

The elections are truly the hour of triumph for India's democratic traditions, which have set high standards for other countries to follow. At the same time, as one reflects on what Indian democracy has been able to achieve for the people, apart from the right to vote, there is an unavoidable feeling of disappointment and unease. As soon as the elections are over and a new government takes office (of whatever complexion and colour), the government becomes a power unto itself. The people's interests tend to be overtaken by the power of special interests and, in political scientist Mancur Olson's famous term, 'distributional coalitions'. These coalitions are generally more interested in influencing the distribution of wealth and income in their favour, rather than in the generation of additional output for the benefit of the public. Ministers and their bureaucrats become authoritarian, self-centred and autocratic. They are no doubt subject to some checks and balances by Parliament and the judiciary but, by and large, they are able to do as they wish. Their accountability to the public is also more apparent than real—at least until the next elections.

Thus, in the words of Pratap Bhanu Mehta, a well-known writer on law and governance in India, 'The broad framework within which practices of popular authorization can be carried out remain intact, but politics itself has become an area where norms exist only in their breach . . . The very mechanism, designed to secure the liberty, well-being and dignity of citizens, representative democracy, is routinely throwing up forces that threaten to undermine it; the very laws that are supposed to enshrine republican aspirations are incapable of commanding minimal respect, and their inaction subjects the entire political process to ridicule. The corruption, mediocrity, indiscipline, venality and lack of moral imagination of the political class, those essential agents of representation in any democracy, make them incapable of attending to the well-being of citizens'.[3]

Ian Little's distinction between the state and the government is crucial in explaining why the nationalist ideals of a state-directed development strategy as an essential component of political democracy did not achieve much. The powers of the state, enshrined in the Constitution, were exercised by the government in office. The government generally represented the interests of a political party (or a coalition of political parties). Political parties, in turn, represented the special interests of a section of the people rather than the country as a whole. In theory, under the Constitution, the responsibility for the policies and actions of the government and its cabinet was 'collective'. However, the prime minister or the chief minister had unfettered discretion in appointing his or her cabinet in consultation with a few top leaders of the party or parties in power. As a result, ministers, once appointed, enjoyed complete powers in respect of the business of their respective ministries as long as they enjoyed the confidence of the leader of their party.

A question that continues to puzzle most observers of the Indian scene is: Why do the people of India, who have the right to vote freely and elect their own government, not exercise greater vigilance over the conduct of their elected representatives? Why do they continue to elect corrupt persons, several of them with criminal records and narrow interests? In several states, with a large number of seats in Parliament, and which have such a decisive role in the formation of the government, a sizeable proportion of the electorate continues to support leaders and parties with an abysmal record of service to the people and little commitment to the growth and development of their respective states. The answer to these questions perhaps really lies in the large incidence of illiteracy—particularly female illiteracy—in several states. According to available statistics, in some states, more than half the voters, and nearly two-thirds of the female voters, are illiterate. As a result, the local parties and political leaders are able to exploit caste, religious or regional factors to their own advantage. This underscores the importance of implementing the country's commitment to provide 'education for all' as a fundamental right. Literacy and education will not totally eliminate the importance of caste and religion in India, but it will certainly make the voters better informed and political parties more accountable.

India has a parliamentary system of government, and the government is expected to continue in office as long as it enjoys the confidence of the majority of the elected members in the Lok Sabha (the House of the People). While in office, the government is accountable to both Houses of Parliament, the Lok Sabha and the Council of States (the Rajya Sabha). The judiciary, with the Supreme Court at its apex, is independent of both the government and Parliament, and its legal pronouncements are binding on all institutions of the state and the public. It is also the custodian of the people's rights and the freedom of the press, as guaranteed in the Constitution.

This is the theory. In practice, the accountability of the government to Parliament and the legislatures is perfunctory and minimal. The relevant rules of business, including regular question hours and calling attention motions, are duly in place and punctiliously observed by the government. However, as long as the government and the parties represented in it have the majority support in Parliament, they can literally get away with anything, including ministerial corruption and the harassment of persons who oppose them. Political parties, small and large, are firmly under the control of their leaders, and inner-party democracy is conspicuous by its absence from most parties. Therefore, by and large, the government is accountable only to a handful of leaders of the parties that are represented in the government. Ironically, in multiparty coalition governments in the states and at the Centre, small local-party formations, with a pronounced loyalty to a particular caste or sect, can have a disproportionate influence in determining the course of government policies.

In practice, Parliament and the legislatures generally do what the government wants them to do, rather than the other way around. Thus, for example, one of the most important functions of Parliament (which, in fact, was the primary reason for the American Revolution and the adoption of the Bill of Rights) is to approve the budget of the government and its taxation and expenditure proposals. In theory, the government cannot tax or spend without parliamentary or legislative authority. In practice, however, this authority is largely procedural. All expenditure and tax decisions are made by the finance minister, with the approval of the prime minister or chief minister, where necessary. The finance minister would no doubt listen to the debate in Parliament and graciously amend some of the budgetary provisions, but, by and large, parliamentary approval is a mere formality.

The government's real accountability to the judiciary is also minimal. In interpreting the constitutional provisions relating to the legislative powers of the government or the division of powers between the Centre and the states, judicial powers are supreme. The judiciary can determine the process through which a government decision has to be legitimized (for example, through parliamentary approval). Its judgements in respect of public interest petitions filed by citizens or dealing with the rights of individuals, particularly civil servants, are also binding. Nevertheless, a determined government can more or less do what it wants—except change the basic structure of the Constitution. It has unfettered powers to have new legislations passed as long as it has the majority, and, except under very exceptional circumstances, these statutory provisions are binding on the judiciary. So far as economic policies are concerned, the government's powers are virtually unlimited, provided appropriate business rules and legislative procedures have been followed.

The long delays in processing cases have further eroded the powers of the judiciary. Such delays are now legendary, and have been further compounded by the almost-limitless powers of the government to notify 'rules' under Acts passed by Parliament or legislatures. The actual statutory provisions, as approved by Parliament, may provide for 'due process' and accountability. However, all acts enacted by Parliament generally have an omnibus provision, whereby the government is free to make 'rules' under the relevant act through executive notifications.

As Amartya Sen has so eloquently argued in his writings and speeches over the years, for the people of India, democracy is its own reward, and the benefits of freedom cannot be judged solely in terms of its contribution to growth or economic well-being. In any case, recent empirical research has established that there is no direct association between success in growth or poverty alleviation and the form of government. Authoritarian governments are as prone to economic failure, if not more, as democracies. At the same time, as Sen has also observed, valuable as democracy is, as a major source of social opportunity, there is a strong need to examine the ways and means of making it function well and realize its full potential. Eternal vigilance on the part of the people is indeed the price of liberty. There is no room for complacency on this score.

On the whole, despite some weaknesses in the working of India's political system on the ground, the opportunities for the country to accelerate its rate of growth further (to, say, 8 per cent or more) and eliminate poverty by improving the public delivery system are much better in the twenty-first century than at any other time in the last half-century. Part of the reason for this resurgence of confidence in India's future is no doubt the process of economic reforms initiated since 1991. However, there is also another important reason why there has been such a dramatic shift in India's economic outlook. The basic reason is that the sources of comparative advantage of nations are vastly different now than they were fifty or even twenty years ago. There are very few developing countries that are as well placed as India to take advantage of the phenomenal changes that have occurred in production technologies, international trade, capital movement and the deployment of skilled manpower. As a result, India today has the knowledge and the skills to produce and process a wide variety of products and services at competitive costs.

While India's opportunities and capabilities are comparatively large, it is also true that the country's actual efforts in alleviating poverty and providing the minimum essential social services to the people have been abysmal. The best-known and internationally recognized measure of socio-economic progress is the Human Development Index (HDI), which is computed annually by the United Nations Development Programme (UNDP). The HDI is a composite of several basic components of human development, such as life expectancy, literacy, standard of living and health. It is believed to be a more comprehensive measure of progress than the per capita income or GDP. According to this index, in 2015, India's rank was 135 among the 187 countries globally. In other words, India figured among the bottom one-third of the countries in terms of human development, notwithstanding the fact that in terms of the overall growth rate of the GDP, India was among the fastest-growing developing countries in the world in the last three decades.

Why is there this sharp and persistent 'disjuncture' between growth and human development, notwithstanding the universally acclaimed economic reforms of 1991? Growth and reforms are obviously not ends in themselves, particularly in a vibrant democracy—'of the people, by the people, and for the people'—like India's. High growth and reforms are 'means' to achieve the end of providing the basic components of human development, especially nutrition, health and literacy, to the people, irrespective of their levels of income.

By and large, all observers of the Indian economy, including governments in power, also generally agree that in order to realize its full potential in the new global environment, it is necessary for India to make a decisive move towards deeper reforms and reduce the pervasive procedural and administrative bottlenecks. Under the new government elected in 2014, while there is agreement in principle for a new policy orientation, looking at the past record, it is not yet clear whether India will, in the next ten to fifteen years, be able to fully seize the opportunities that are now available. There are primarily three factors that are likely to impede India's progress: the deadweight of the past, the power of distributional coalitions and the growing disjuncture between economics and politics.

Even after more than half a century of development experience, India's vision of the future continues to be clouded by beliefs that have failed to yield expected results in terms of growth, investment and savings. In view of the colonial experience of foreign domination, economic stagnation and increasing poverty, the post-Independence development strategy had given very high priority to making India economically independent. Based on the Soviet experience, it was believed that economic independence and high domestic savings could be achieved only if the 'commanding heights' of the economy were in the hands of the public sector. It was assumed that if the means of production were owned by the state, all the value added in production would flow to the people. As a result, public savings are likely to increase. These savings could then be used for further investment and growth, and India would soon be able to catch up with the developed world. This was a most heart-warming economic vision, supported by the leading economists of the day and widely respected academic models of savings, investment and growth.

However, it soon became evident that instead of generating savings, the public sector had become a drain on public savings. Despite its occupying the 'commanding heights', by the end of the 1990s, public-sector savings were negative by as much as 4 per cent of the GDP. These negative savings led to the fast accumulation of internal public debt and lower investment than usual. In the annals of development history, it is hard to find another example of a perfectly sensible idea—the need for higher public investment for greater public good—leading to exactly the opposite result: higher public consumption with diminishing returns for the public!

Why did such unrealistic assumptions about the sources of growth in public savings and investment persist for so long? Ever since Independence, India was fortunate enough to have a string of top development economists and thinkers available to advise the government in the process of planning and economic policy formulation—among them were well-known names like Prof. P.C. Mahalanobis, Dr Pitambar Pant and Prof. Raj Krishna. Yet, the results in terms of social or economic development—leaving aside the most recent period—were disappointing. Part of the reason for this sorry state of affairs was that economic and development strategy, propounded by the best economic brains and enshrined in successive Five-Year Plans, seldom reflected the political and administrative realities on the ground. The political assumption underlying the favoured economic strategy was that the control over allocation of the country's savings by elected politicians would ensure that all such savings were used to promote the best interests of the country's poor in the most efficient manner. The administrative assumption was that the required bureaucratic response to implement the government's development programmes would be forthcoming in abundant measure. The system of administration at the different levels was expected to work in complete harmony, delivering savings and investments as postulated in the development models and implementing government programmes as planned.

These political and administrative assumptions, unfortunately, turned out to be unrealistic. Nevertheless, as it so often happens, theories once propounded and accepted as ideal are difficult to discard, even if the results turn out to be different from what was expected. Various alibis for unsatisfactory outcomes are usually advanced to justify the initial choice of strategy, accompanied by exhortations for better performance in the future. There is also a marked tendency among distinguished development theorists, both on the left and the right, to take ideological positions on such matters as planning and the appropriate role of the state in the economy, without fully taking into account the country's institutional structure, its social realities and the global environment.

The hangover of the past is also reflected in the continuing dominant role of the bureaucracy in determining policy outcomes. It must be said to the credit of India's planners that as early as 1956, the Second Plan did ask itself the question whether the civil service would prove equal to the tasks assigned to it by the Plan. The subsequent Plans also expressed their desperation about widespread administrative inefficiencies and bottlenecks that were slowing down the economy. However, this desperation was not reflected in the actual allocation of public resources or in the growth of administrative expenditure. India went on adding newer, larger and more comprehensive schemes to tackle national problems in virtually every walk of life, calling for greater and greater administrative involvement.

Thus, although there has been substantial policy liberalization in respect of corporate investments in the economy during the 1990s, the regulatory and administrative processes that are required for the various kinds of approvals (from land acquisition to environmental clearance), by and large, continue to remain. There are multiple government agencies in place, which work at cross purposes with each other. The number of permissions required to set up an industry as well as the number of inspectors involved in the bargaining process of granting such permissions have, in fact, increased over the years.

The procedural complexity and administrative apathy are widely known and appreciated even at the higher levels of the government. However, it has not been feasible to bring about any systematic improvement because of the immense power of the coalition of special interests that benefited greatly from the old strategy of centralized control at the expense of the general public. Political leaders gained—and are still gaining—from their control over the resources of the public-sector enterprises, their power to regulate the activities of large private-sector enterprises, their power to fix the prices of agricultural and industrial goods, and their ability to provide subsidies and incur fiscal deficits. Workers in the organized sector, in both the public and the private sectors, gained from the immense powers and political patronage enjoyed by them. Bureaucrats gained from opportunities for corruption at different levels in the administration, and statutorily guaranteed security for their jobs. Private-sector entrepreneurs and contractors gained from their ability to influence government decisions in their favour through higher protection or preferential contracts, particularly during elections, which were taking place with increasing frequency.

These coalitions of special interests ensured that the necessary change in the initial development strategy did not occur for as long as possible, and when it became unavoidable (due to external crises), it was slow and politically controversial. An understanding of this past experience is necessary so that its repetition can be avoided in the future. India must be willing and ready to change its strategy and policies when initial conditions have changed. This can happen only if public policy, *ab initio,* guards against the emergence and entrenchment of special interests by limiting governmental and bureaucratic powers.

Another phenomenon that is likely to impede economic progress is the growing disjuncture between economics and politics in India. It is increasingly evident that despite the spread of political democracy to all parts of India, which is a laudable achievement, a government's performance in regard to the growth rate or alleviation of poverty is not an important factor in determining electoral outcomes. Thus, in the past, governments that performed relatively well economically lost elections at the Centre (for example, the Congress government in 1996, or the coalition led by the Bharatiya Janata Party in 2004). Similarly, states that performed very poorly in economic terms or in implementing anti-poverty programmes continued to return to power parties that were responsible for this state of affairs.

Governance and Corruption

During Independence, India inherited a colonial state and kept much of its governance structure intact. By all accounts, during this period, the administrative structure devised by the British was efficient in meeting its limited objectives. It was highly authoritarian and remote so far as the general public was concerned. Its primary purpose was to maintain law and order and promote Britain's trading interests as per the laws enacted by the British. The same governance architecture was asked to bear the full load of centralized planning and a multitude of public programmes after Independence. With rising expectations and the failure to deliver what was promised in the second and subsequent Plans, newer and more comprehensive government schemes were introduced in virtually every walk of life. These posed new administrative challenges in an environment of diminishing fiscal resources, periodic external crises and mounting procedural complexities.

As the administrative system became less efficient and more complex, requiring more and more public servants to perform the same tasks, it acquired a momentum of its own. With rising wages, periodic Pay Commissions and judicial pronouncements in favour of government employees, the so-called public servants soon became their own masters, with little accountability to the people or their representatives. As government service became the most attractive source of employment, the vested interests of politicians and power brokers ensured that more and more schemes and public programmes were added to the existing ones. Over time, the creation of government jobs became an end in itself, and administrative salaries and pensions became the main component of most schemes.

Despite some recent changes, the civil service continues to suffer from a myriad problems, which have accumulated over a number of decades. While job security is still very much present at all levels, the sense of financial security has changed at the different levels of various services. The top levels, while low in number, feel less secure than before in view of the widening gap between monetary compensation in civil services and the private sector. The lower rungs of the service, which account for the vast majority of the employees, enjoy compensation that is twice as high as the equivalent levels in the private organized sector. Higher-level jobs are transferable across the country as well as between departments, while lower-level jobs are non-transferable. Tenures have become shorter for transferable jobs, while access to various requirements, such as housing or education, have become more difficult. The combined effect of all these pulls and pressures is that the government and public-sector jobs have become progressively less attractive at the top but immensely more attractive at the clerical levels, because alternative employment opportunities have shrunk, partly as a result of antiquated labour laws.

The decay in the country's administrative and public delivery systems affected the poor the most. They are critically dependent on the availability of public services and essential infrastructure, particularly in the rural areas where 700 million or more people live. A redefinition of the powers and the roles of ministers and civil servants in decision-making processes, and their accountability for performance, are essential if India is to succeed in eliminating the worst forms of poverty in the midst of plenty.

At the ministerial level, a new institutional and constitutional initiative is required to hold individual ministers accountable for the efficient delivery of public services and anti-poverty programmes. Fortunately, the present government has initiated some new initiatives to assess the actual action taken by the different ministries in respect of their achievements, goals and removing bottlenecks in implementation. Earlier ministers (such as those responsible for rural development, water resources, health and anti-poverty programmes) were quick to announce ambitious annual or five-year targets for the benefit of the poor. However, no minister was actually held accountable (or censured) for poor performance. The reason for the non-accountability of individual ministers was the cherished doctrine of 'collective responsibility' of the council of ministers in a parliamentary form of government. In theory, the notion is that the government, as a whole, must resign if it loses the confidence of Parliament, and not just the non-performing minister. This hallowed doctrine, which evolved in the nineteenth century in Britain, lost much of its relevance in India in view of the vast expansion of government activity in economic areas and the increase in the power of individual ministers. Now, the government is not only in charge of laying down the broad contours of macroeconomic policies but also for implementing a whole host of projects and programmes at the micro level. Individual ministers can take virtually all decisions affecting public enterprises or projects under their charge. As such, it is important to hold them accountable for the outcome.

So far as the civil service structure is concerned, taking into account past experience and the failure to implement the reports and recommendations of numerous commissions, study groups and committees, it is necessary to recognize that it is simply not feasible to reform the system from within. The only solution is to reduce the direct role of the bureaucracy in the management of public services. Thus, case studies by several independent agencies have shown that in every case where the management of a public service was contracted out to private groups or enterprises, the distribution and quality of the service improved and the net cost to the public was reduced. In India also there have been successful examples of 'micro-privatization' (such as the Sulabh Sauchalayas and Public Call Offices). These initiatives need to be replicated in respect of other services.

In addition to the need for improving the administrative system for the delivery of public services, there is the larger question of the reform of the civil service apparatus for better governance of the country. The most critical issue that needs to be tackled is the 'motivational' issue at the higher levels of the civil services. With transfers being effected at very short notice at the instance of ministers, the tendency among civil servants is that, in order to survive, it is best to conform to ministerial wishes, however unsustainable. It is necessary to lay down some transparent ground rules for the transfers of civil servants before three or five years in a particular post. Within the executive branch, there is also the need for 'separation of powers' between the ministers and civil servants in so far as postings, transfers, promotions and other administrative matters are concerned.

It is sad, to say the least, that a country with India's rich cultural heritage and political history has one of the worst rankings in the Corruption Perception Index and Global Corruption Barometer compiled by Transparency International. In 2015, India's rank in the Corruption Index was 38 on a scale of 0 to 100, where zero is supposed to be totally corrupt and 100 is very clean. Regrettably, there is also widespread public acceptance of corruption as an unavoidable aspect of Indian life. It is not widely realized, however, that corruption is one of the primary reasons for low productivity of investments, fiscal drain and continued mass poverty. High corruption is associated with the wrong choice of high-cost public projects, low-maintenance expenditure and poor quality of essential public infrastructure, which, in turn, increases the cost of production of goods and services by business enterprises, both public and private.

An important finding of empirical research is that the adverse effects of corruption are more pronounced on small enterprises and on the growth of employment in the economy. Thus, some years ago, a survey of 3000 enterprises across twenty transition economies, covering all regions, found that corruption and anti-competitive practices were perceived as the most difficult obstacles by start-up firms. For small enterprises, such practices raised costs and reduced profits because they had to make payments that did not contribute to productivity or output, but were necessary for survival. In order to avoid undue harassment, bribes amounting to a substantial portion of the operating costs had to be paid to meet the demands of a host of inspectors working in concert with each other.

To improve productivity, reduce incentives for launching high-cost projects and alleviate poverty, a multipronged strategy to reduce the scope for corruption is an urgent necessity.

Under the present government, there has been substantial progress in weeding out large-scale corruption at the top level. Measures like government tendering through e-auctions and government-to-government coordination for large procurements from abroad have also helped in reducing the scope of corruption. An effective strategy to further reduce corruption would need to focus on institutional reform as well as on reducing the 'demand' and 'supply' of corruption at the lower levels of the administrative structure. On the institutional side, there are multiple investigating and prosecution agencies at the Centre and in the states to fight corruption. However, while a large number of cases are under investigation at any point of time, the success in prosecuting and punishing the guilty is conspicuous by its absence. In fact, the multiplicity of agencies and the ease with which investigations can be launched without the need to complete them are among the most important causes of the ineffectiveness of anti-corruption measures. An essential component of an anti-corruption strategy is a reduction in the number of agencies involved in investigation and the number of cases that these agencies are expected to investigate. No more than a handful of major cases should be referred for investigation, and the agencies involved should have sufficient access to funds and technical expertise to launch prosecution within ninety days of receiving a major complaint. The objective should be to provide deterrence and exemplary punishment in a few cases rather than to investigate a multitude of cases without any result.

In order to further reduce the supply of corruption, it is necessary to reduce the protection provided to government servants and other public functionaries under the Constitution and various judicial pronouncements. Two statutory provisions, among several others, which deserve to be amended forthwith, are: Article 311 of the Constitution of India and the Official Secrets Act (1923). Article 311, and the subsequent judicial verdicts, provide virtually unlimited protection to corrupt civil servants, because of elaborate and complicated legal requirements before such an official can be reduced in rank, let alone dismissed from service or sent to prison. In order to reduce the level of protection provided to civil servants, it is essential to remove all cases of corruption from the purview of Article 311. This is the minimum that needs to be done.

Another vital area on the 'supply' side that requires immediate legislative action is the state-funding of political parties. The matter has often been discussed but no feasible and politically acceptable consensus has emerged. While recognizing that an equitable formula for the allocation of budgetary funds among multiple parties of different sizes is intrinsically difficult, it should still be possible to evolve a formula that is fair and reasonable. What is necessary now, when a majority government is in power at the Centre, is to find the necessary political consensus to move in this direction.

The demand for corruption has a 'retail' component and a 'wholesale' component. The retail component consists of the demand generated by individuals who require various kinds of permissions to carry on with the ordinary business of life. The wholesale component is generated by self-seeking corporates and businesses to take advantage of a restrictive practice or price control for their profit. With liberalization of the economy, the demand for wholesale corruption has been reduced, but it is still quite high because of a large number of clearances that are required at various levels, and the large number of ministries and agencies that are involved in providing such permissions.

In order to curb the demand for corruption, the most immediate priority is to 'outsource' and decentralize the system of providing various kinds of licenses, registration and permissions to the general public. An example of such outsourcing in a routine and simple matter, which has substantially reduced petty corruption and delays, is the decision by the Income Tax Department to issue Permanent Account Numbers (PAN) for tax payments by citizens on the Internet. Further outsourcing of such routine functions among the different autonomous agencies can lead to greater accountability and responsiveness to the needs of the public, and can help reduce corruption. Similarly, in order to reduce the wholesale component in the demand for corruption, it is essential to simplify administrative procedures, reduce the number of governmental agencies involved in providing clearances and rely on self-certification (with adequate safeguards) by corporate and businesses, in compliance with regulatory and legal requirements. The procedural simplification introduced in recent years in foreign-exchange transactions and the elimination of the need for case-by-case clearances has virtually eliminated corruption in such transactions. Some years ago, this was an area where corruption was rampant. The illegal market in foreign exchange has also virtually disappeared.

There is, of course, a great deal more that can be done in the future to further the governance system and reduce corruption in the country. If we succeed in reducing administrative complexity and political discretion, the rest will be relatively easy to accomplish.

Concluding Observation

By the mid-1990s India had successfully embarked on a programme of economic reforms and, for the first time after 1956, achieved security in its balance-of-payments position. As one looks back to 1991 and the developments since then in India and abroad, two facts about the evolution of India's economic policies are striking. The first is that India was able to avoid the recurrence of a crisis during the 1990s, when a number of robust and fast-growing developing and other countries experienced their worst financial crises. This group of countries included Mexico, Argentina, Brazil, Russia and, of course, the East Asian countries including Japan. The reason why India, despite its relatively weak economy, was able to avoid a financial crisis in the 1990s was due to its ability to undertake reforms with caution and pragmatism, without falling into the trap of 'ideological certainty' and making changes (such as capital account convertibility under conditions of global volatile exchange rate regimes) advocated by many distinguished experts and international institutions. India was quick to realize that while the integration of the global financial markets and advances in technology provided substantial new opportunities, developing countries had also become subject to greater vulnerability and external shocks. India, therefore, took a number of measures to minimize its vulnerability to external crises. These policies proved highly successful, and by the end of the decade, India emerged as a country with one of the strongest external sectors in the developing world.

The second striking fact about the evolution of India's economic policies in the 1990s is that, despite its record of successful macroeconomic management, India was unable to make much progress in the areas of institutional and administrative reforms, which were vital for sustainable high growth. Several distinguished economists and planners, from time to time, have suggested a programme of action for accelerating India's growth and development on a sustainable basis. These suggestions have included policy proposals to improve external and domestic competition; eliminate direct physical controls on production and trade by corporate as well as public enterprises; impose a 'hard budget' constraint on public-sector enterprises (so that the losses of public-sector enterprises are not financed by the government); further reduce fiscal deficit; and improve the balance-of-payments viability by adopting a realistic exchange rate policy and shifting the incentive structure in favour of exports. It is perhaps reasonable to say that in all these areas, the progress of reforms in India in the last two decades has been noteworthy, while the results have been better than expected.

In addition to these policy measures, there is now an urgent need to decentralize the decision-making processes from secretariats and ministries to local institutions and enterprises, reduce the size of the state, make the administrative system more functional and achieve full literacy as early as possible. The main task, even after so many years of progress, continues to be the need to launch a bold programme of reforms in the role of the state and the governance structure.

In this respect, an important priority for the future is to redefine the primary role of the government in the economy.

At the macroeconomic level, the political (i.e., ministerial) role of the government should be to ensure a stable and competitive environment, with a strong external sector and a transparent domestic financial system. While the macroeconomic priorities (for example, the so-called trade-off between growth and inflation) may be decided by the government, the instrumentalities for achieving these objectives must be left to autonomous regulatory and promotional agencies. Similarly, the government's direct role in economic areas should be reset in favour of ensuring the availability of public goods (such as roads and water) and essential services (such as health and education) to the people. In these areas, the government's role must expand substantially. At the same time, its role in managing commercial enterprises deserves to be correspondingly reduced. The latter objective should be achieved without affecting, in any way, the financial and other benefits of those who are presently employed.

Towards the end of the twentieth century, there were two interesting prognostications about India's potential. The first was by a professor of business management in the United States (Rosenzweig, 1998).[4] He estimated that by 2025, India would be the third-largest economy in the world (after the United States and China). The second projection was by a well-known Indian economist (Parikh, 1999).[5] It was projected that India would reach a per capita income of US $30,000 or higher by 2047, making it one of the fastest-growing countries in the world.

Since the beginning of the twenty-first century, the confidence about India's economic prospects is gratifying. There is no doubt that India now has an opportunity to achieve high growth and remove the worst forms of poverty in the foreseeable future. At the same time, it is useful to emphasize that this is not the first time that India's economic prospects are considered to be highly positive. In the early 1950s, soon after Independence, India had won worldwide admiration for initiating the process of development planning within a democratic framework. Similarly, in the early 1970s (after the Bangladesh War), and in the mid-1980s (with the resurgence of savings and investment) India was believed to have entered a new growth path. However, these new opportunities did not last long, and the economy was plunged into prolonged crises after some time. The fundamentals are no doubt stronger now, but India still faces some old and new challenges in the areas of politics and governance. These challenges can only be met if India is able to generate sufficient political will to pursue the right policies and shake off the deadweight of the past. Hopefully, despite several challenges, India's participative and democratic system will ensure that corrective action to make India's economy stronger and its politics more people-oriented will be forthcoming sooner rather than later.

7

Separation of Powers: The Myth and the Reality*

The debate about the doctrine of separation of powers, and exactly what it involves, is as old as the Constitution itself. It was extensively debated in the Constituent Assembly and has also figured in various judgements handed down by the Supreme Court after the Constitution was adopted. Although the controversy about defining the precise boundaries of the powers of the different institutions has recurred from time to time, there is, nonetheless, a broad agreement among all concerned on some fundamental points.

Thus, the doctrine of separation of powers is acknowledged as an integral part of the basic features of our Constitution. It is also commonly agreed that all the three organs of the

---

* Based on the Nani A. Palkhiwala Memorial Lecture, Mumbai, 16 January 2006; and Chapters 4 and 5 of my book *India's Politics: A View from the Backbench* (New Delhi: Penguin, 2007).

state, i.e., the legislature, the judiciary and the executive, are bound by and subject to the provisions of the Constitution, which demarcates their respective powers, jurisdictions, responsibilities and relationships with one another. It is assumed that none of the organs of the state, including the judiciary, would exceed its powers as laid down in the Constitution. It is also expected that in the overall interest of the country, even though their jurisdictions are separated and demarcated, all the institutions would work in harmony and in tandem to maximize the public good.

The issue of the relative jurisdictional boundaries of the organs of the state, however, acquired a new momentum in 2005. During state elections in early 2005, in some states, particularly Jharkhand, Goa and Bihar, no party or coalition of parties had a clear majority. The situation was further complicated by the fact that neither the governors of these states (who had the final powers to appoint a government) nor the presiding officers of the legislatures (who had the powers to conduct the proceedings of the House where the majority claimed by a new government was to be tested) were considered to be impartial in their decisions. Irrespective of the intrinsic merits of the decisions taken by any of these constitutional authorities, an appeal to the courts by the aggrieved parties, therefore, became unavoidable.

Thus, in Jharkhand, after the elections in March 2005, the Governor was pleased to swear in a government headed by a member of the Union cabinet, who did not appear to have a clear majority. He was also given a number of days to prove his majority on the floor of the House. The Opposition parties, who claimed to have a majority, were extremely upset by this decision of the Governor and filed a writ petition in the Supreme Court challenging his decision. In March 2005, the court passed an order that, inter alia, directed the Speaker to extend the assembly session by a day and conduct a floor test between the contending political alliances. In light of the court's decision, the earlier government formed by the Union minister decided to tender its resignation on the advice of the Central government. An alternative government was then formed by a combination of other parties that was able to prove its majority on the floor of the House.

The directions of the Supreme Court to the Speaker of the Jharkhand assembly raised a legal storm, as these were interpreted by several experts as an intrusion into the jurisdiction of the legislature. This view was also endorsed by a Conference of the Presiding Officers of Legislative Bodies of India, convened at short notice in March 2005 to deliberate on the constitutional issue arising from the verdict of the Supreme Court. In no uncertain terms, the presiding officers expressed their concern over 'such orders passed by the courts repeatedly which tend to disturb the delicate balance of power between Judiciary and Legislature and appear to be a transgression into the independence of the Parliamentary System of our Country'.

In May 2005, the controversy relating to the Supreme Court's directions in the Jharkhand case acquired a new dimension. This time, it related to the action taken by the President of India to dissolve the Bihar assembly on the recommendation of the Governor of the state, and the advice of the Union cabinet. The state had been under President's rule for a few months, and the assembly was in suspended animation as no party or combination of parties had emerged with a clear majority in the earlier elections in February 2005. Legislators belonging to a few minority parties had become restive, and there were strong rumours that some of them were likely to join a coalition of parties opposed to the previous ruling party in the state, which was a member of the ruling coalition at the Centre. On the grounds of alleged 'horse-trading' among legislators, the Governor decided to recommend the dissolution of the assembly to the Union cabinet and, through it, to the President, who was then on a state visit to Moscow. The recommendation was duly accepted late at night in Moscow, and the assembly was dissolved. Some affected legislators filed a case against the action taken by the executive branch.

The Centre's legal position in this case, as filed in an affidavit before the Supreme Court, was that the Court is not to enquire—rather, it is not concerned with—whether any advice was tendered by any minister or council of ministers to the President, and if so, what was that advice. That is a matter between the President and his council of ministers. In other words, according to the government's view, the council of ministers could advise the President to pass any order (irrespective of its merits); the President had no option but to accept that advice under the Constitution, and the court had no right to examine whether the action of the executive was legal or not.

After hearing the arguments, in October 2005, the Supreme Court gave a summary verdict declaring the action of the Central government in dissolving the Bihar assembly as being 'unconstitutional' and unreasonable. The court, however, did not order the revival of the old assembly as fresh elections had been announced by the Election Commission and were scheduled to take place within a few days. The court's verdict caused considerable public embarrassment to the government, since the decision to dissolve the assembly was taken by the President at very short notice, on the advice of the Union cabinet.

The Diminishing Role of Parliament

The functioning of Parliament and state legislatures after 1989 was examined in detail by the National Commission to Review the Constitution in 2002. The Commission's observations are worth noting:

> If there is a sense of unease with the way the Parliament and the State legislatures are functioning, it may be due to a decline in recent years in both the quantity and quality of work done by them . . . Even the relatively fewer days on which the houses meet are often marked by unseemly incidents, including use of force to intimidate opponents, shouting and shutting out of debate and discussion resulting in frequent adjournments. There is increasing concern about the decline of Parliament, falling standards of debate, erosion of the moral authority and prestige of the supreme tribune of the people.[1]

Over time, as it happens, the diminishing role of Parliament in the conduct of national affairs has become broader than what was highlighted by the commission in the above passage. In the context of coalition politics, there is also increasing acceptance by political leaders of the frequent violation of democratic norms and conventions in the political decision-making process. In the annals of India's long and distinguished parliamentary history, the events that took place over five days, between 18 and 22 March, during the 2006 Budget session, were perhaps unique. Over the course of these five days, a number of unexpected decisions were announced by the government regarding the business agendas of the two Houses, which were passively accepted by both the Houses. These decisions involved a major change in the established procedure for consideration of the Budget, a drastic revision in the business of the two Houses without adequate notice and a sudden adjournment of Parliament *sine die* (followed by a reversal of this decision again a few days later). The ready acceptance by Parliament, the supreme institution of India's democracy, of decisions that were contrary to well-established parliamentary conventions, has had serious consequences for the functioning of Parliament in recent years. It is, therefore, worth going into the events of these five days in March 2006 in some detail.

As per the usual procedure, the Budget session of Parliament for 2006 was convened by the President to meet in two parts—from 16 February to 17 March and again from 3 April to 28 April. However, on 7 March 2006, in view of the elections announced by the Election Commission in five states over the months of April and May, it was decided to have a longer interval between the two parts of the Budget session. The dates announced earlier for the two parts of the session were changed, and it was decided to hold the first session from 16 February to 22 March, and the second session from 10 to 23 May. The first part was longer and the second part was a bit shorter than the original schedule, but on the whole, the entire Budget session was supposed to be long enough to permit the examination of the Budget as per established convention.

According to Rules 272 and 331G of the Rules of Procedure and Conduct of Business in the Rajya Sabha and the Lok Sabha, respectively, it is mandatory for the demands for grants of the ministries and departments of the Government of India to be examined by the concerned standing committees of Parliament (which were set up in 1993). The standing committees consist of members of both Houses of Parliament. The agenda and the meetings of the committees are conducted by a chairperson, who is normally a senior member of one of the Houses. The examination of the Budget grants by these committees allows members, belonging to both Houses and to different parties, to question the senior representatives of the ministries or departments, and also to hear and examine other witnesses, including members of non-governmental organizations and experts. The reports of these committees on matters under their purview, including the Budget demands, are submitted to the two Houses of Parliament for consideration.

On 18 March 2006, the government decided to introduce a motion in the Rajya Sabha for the suspension of Rule 272 (and a similar motion for the suspension of the relevant rule in the Lok Sabha). The motion to suspend the consideration of Budget demands by the standing committees was moved and adopted without discussion in the two Houses on the same day. With the suspension of consideration by the standing committees, the ground was cleared for the adoption of the Budget as well as the Finance Bill in the first part of the session itself. The Lok Sabha decided to approve the Budget demand for grants (or the Appropriation Bill) on 18 March, followed by the approval of the Rajya Sabha on 20 March. On the next day, 21 March, the Finance Bill was also approved without any discussion, and the Parliament was adjourned *sine die*. This was an extraordinary and unprecedented event in a year when there was no change of government, no general election and no internal or external emergency. And yet, it was decided to rush the Budget through Parliament without proper consideration and adjourn the session.

After four days of abrupt *sine die* adjournments, the government announced its intention of reconvening Parliament, as earlier scheduled, from 10–23 May 2006. A formal notice to this effect was also issued to all members on 5 April 2006, after the necessary formalities had been completed. On 28 March 2006, members were also informed that, notwithstanding the completion of discussion and voting on the Demands for Grants of the respective Ministries/Departments for the year 2006–07 by the Lok Sabha, it was decided that the Department-related Parliamentary Standing Committees would examine these Demands for Grants and present their reports to the respective Houses.

Thus, the standing committees were also resurrected as suddenly as they had been dispensed with, even though there was nothing left for them to consider, recommend or approve. This move was yet another step in the direction of the diminishing role of Parliament in the conduct of the nation's affairs.

The Executive and the Judiciary

According to Article 75 of the Constitution of India, 'The Council of Ministers shall be collectively responsible to the House of the People.' However, as mentioned above, the responsibility of the Council of Ministers to the House of the People or the Parliament of India is largely pro forma. As the events of the five days, 18–22 March, abundantly demonstrated, as long as a government can command the support of a majority of members belonging to one or more parties, it is the will of the government that prevails in Parliament rather than the other way round.

In the earlier era of coalition governments, consisting of parties with different political agendas, the notion of the collective responsibility of the Council of Ministers had also suffered. Ministers were inclined to push forward their own interests or party priorities without informing the Cabinet. The erosion of collective responsibility was accompanied by a process of politicization of the permanent civil services. The old notion that the civil services should render impartial and apolitical advice to the ministers was abandoned to a large extent. With unlimited powers of transfers and appointments in the hands of government in power, civil servants were fully at their mercy.

Fortunately, the judiciary still continues to be the final arbiter of the legality or otherwise of decisions taken by the executive either on its own or with the approval of Parliament, as required. In the light of the Supreme Court's 1973 decision (in the famous *Kesavananda* case), which confirmed that the 'basic structure' of the Constitution was sacrosanct, the judiciary continues to have the ultimate power to interpret the Constitution and its intent.

The Principle of Collective Responsibility

In the parliamentary system of government, unlike the presidential system, all members of the Cabinet are members of the legislature (the Parliament at the federal level and the state assemblies at the state level). The prime minister is elected to head the government by the party that has won the majority (or is selected by consensus among the parties in a coalition) and is supposed to be the 'first among equals'. The prime minister, in turn, selects the members of the Cabinet and assigns them to different ministries and departments of the government as ministers or ministers of state. The prime minister is also free to create new ministries and departments or merge and change items of business assigned to the different ministries. In the formation of new governments, depending on their personal standing in the party and the extent of political power they enjoy, prime ministers are free to act on their own, or they may need to consult the leader of their party and/or its coalition partners.

Once the decisions concerning the composition of the Council of Ministers have been made and communicated to the President, these decisions are final. The Cabinet is then supposed to be collectively responsible to Parliament or the legislatures. All policy decisions taken by the individual ministries, irrespective of who heads them, and all laws or amendments to existing laws, have to be approved by the Cabinet as a whole before they are introduced in Parliament. All Cabinet decisions, once approved, are unanimous, and the Cabinet is collectively responsible for them.

The principle of collective responsibility of the Cabinet has some important constitutional implications for the conduct of individual ministers. First, no major policy or administrative decision should be taken without appropriate inter-ministerial consultations and the approval of the prime minister. Second, all such decisions must represent a consensus among the members of the Cabinet or its committees, whether they are directly concerned with the subject under consideration or not. Third, all members of the Cabinet are jointly and collectively responsible for the performance of the government in Parliament (and, thus, indirectly to the people), irrespective of the particular ministry to which a particular item of business has been allotted.

An important corollary of the principle of collective responsibility is that no individual minister can be formally held accountable for the failure of a ministry to implement a decision or a programme announced by the government. Thus, to take an extreme example, the government can declare war or sign a peace or border treaty, which may later be considered unwarranted or badly implemented. An individual minister, however, cannot be held responsible for the wrong decision or failure in implementation. The Council of Ministers as a whole—irrespective of any internal dissension and disagreement—would have to rise in defence of the minister. The prime minister or the leader of the party is, of course, free to ask the minister to resign or remove him or her. However, so far as the public or Parliament is concerned, he or she has no formal individual responsibility and accountability for implementing the decisions taken on behalf of the government. An individual minister cannot be censured or suspended by Parliament for any policy or administrative decision taken by his or her ministry with the approval of the Cabinet. Questions may be asked, 'calling attention' motions may be moved and cases may even be filed in courts for impropriety or corruption, but the person can continue in office as long as the prime minister wishes him to and the party in power enjoys a majority in the House.

Against the above background, it is not surprising that successive governments and ministers, since Independence, have announced grand plans for removing poverty, achieving full employment and providing essential services to the people. And yet, India, despite all the recent growth and shine, remains one of the poorest countries in the world, with the highest number of poor persons, who enjoy the right to vote and elect their government. Programmes aimed at removing poverty and providing services to the poor have also been the principal items on the economic agenda of every political party at the time of elections. The instrumentalities and specific policies proposed to be adopted, if voted to power, have varied from one party to another, but the anti-poverty objective has been the same. In view of this, it is surprising that, despite the increasing frequency of elections and the different combinations of parties that have formed governments in recent years, the public delivery system has continued to deteriorate. The poor, of course, continue to have the power to vote, and enjoy substantial electoral power in a majority of constituencies in the country. But once the elections are over, accountability for the performance of ministers is conspicuous by its absence.

While the principle of collective responsibility has effectively shielded individual ministers from being held accountable for the performance of their ministries, in practice, this principle has not prevented them from taking decisions on matters of great public importance without seeking a formal approval of the Cabinet.

In March 2004, for example, when the National Democratic Alliance (NDA) coalition was in power, the then minister in charge of higher education announced the decision of his ministry to drastically reduce the financial autonomy enjoyed by the Indian Institutes of Management (IIMs). This decision, which was taken by the minister without any reference or endorsement of the Cabinet, would have had major implications for the viability of the IIMs, which had contributed significantly to improving corporate governance and competitiveness. The decision of the ministry led to widespread protests by the IIMs and other educational institutions. The ministry then announced that, in order to ensure the financial viability of the IIMs, the government would provide adequate direct subsidy to cover the difference between the cost of providing an education and the amount that the IIMs were going to be allowed to charge by way of fees. In other words, the government was prepared to subsidize even those students who could afford to pay higher fees in order to impose 'price controls' on the IIMs! This decision was also announced without the approval of the Cabinet or the ministry responsible for the Budget (i.e., the Ministry of Finance).

However, before the above decision could be implemented, there was a change in government and a new coalition came to power. In May 2004, the new minister decided to reverse the earlier decision. This was widely welcomed by the IIMs as well as other educational institutions. Thus, two diametrically opposite decisions with serious implications for the future of higher education in India were announced by the same ministry within a space of two months under two different ministers. These decisions reflected their policy preferences and were taken without adequate consultations or discussions with the Cabinet and others concerned with the matter.

Other similar cases, where particular ministers have decided to announce important government decisions on their own, have now become matters of considerable public concern. No one really knows what the collective view of the government is on matters of public importance and the validity of pronouncements by individual ministers on controversial issues. An important issue that requires consideration by a majority government in power, is: If, on the one hand, the Cabinet cannot be assumed to be collectively responsible for ministerial pronouncements and, on the other hand, ministers cannot be held individually responsible, then who should take responsibility for the actions taken (or not taken) on behalf of the government? This question has become even more pertinent in light of the diminishing role of Parliament in enforcing the accountability of the Council of Ministers.

The Politicization of Administration

For many years after Independence, India's civil services were regarded as exemplary among developing nations. Under India's system of public administration, there was supposed to be a clear division of roles between the permanent civil service and the political leadership. The bureaucracy was subordinate to the elected politicians, who were chosen by the prime minister at the Centre (and by the chief ministers in the states) to head different ministries and departments. The government's priorities and its work programme were set by the elected politicians, and the bureaucracy was supposed to ensure that this programme was implemented according to the laws in force and in line with approved administrative procedures. While implementing the programmes set by the Cabinet and the ministers, bureaucrats were expected to act without fear or favour and ensure that the benefits of the programmes flowed to the people regardless of their political affiliations. While the elected politicians were free to overrule the advice rendered by civil servants, the advisory functions of the bureaucracy were expected to be performed without regard to their impact on the private interests of politicians and the party in power.

Over the years, slowly but surely, the role of the bureaucracy has unfortunately been seriously compromised. Thus, the National Commission to Review the Working of the Constitution, in 2002, in addition to highlighting the declining role of Parliament, also pointed out:

> Arbitrary and questionable methods of appointments, promotions and transfers of officers by political superiors also led to corrosion of the moral basis of its independence. It has strengthened the temptation in services to collusive practices with politicians to avoid the inconvenience of transfers and for officers to gain advantages by ingratiating themselves to political masters. They would do the politicians' biddings rather than adhere to rules. Lest the situation becomes more vicious, it is necessary that a better arrangement be conceived under the Constitution.[2]

The deleterious effects of frequent transfers on the morale and effectiveness of top civil servants have been substantial. The costs to the country in terms of the loss of quality of administration have also been significant. Administration has become increasingly weak and arbitrary, since there is no time available to a newly appointed civil servant to acquire even the minimum knowledge necessary for an effective discharge of functions. Incompetence at the top leads to acts of passive resistance and delays by subordinates. Corruption becomes unavoidable, both to avoid transfers as well as to secure remunerative postings by corrupt officials.

The common experience of most citizens who have to deal with a government agency for any purpose, large and small, is that of insuperable problems and delays. There is also a large diversion of funds from the intended purposes to bureaucrats, politicians and middlemen at various levels of the administrative hierarchy. Thus, in a memorable and widely quoted observation, after visiting some important development programmes several years ago, Prime Minister Rajiv Gandhi had pointed out that: 'Out of Rs 100 crore allocated to an anti-poverty project, I know that only Rs 15 crore reaches the people. The remainder is gobbled up by middlemen, power brokers, contractors and the corrupt.'[3]

A host of recommendations for improving the system have been made by numerous high-powered committees. However, the general view among experts and experienced civil servants now seems to be that the reform of the system is not feasible. This is not because the country does not know what to do but because of the political resistance to the reform of the civil service. Thus, a former Cabinet Secretary has written in his memoirs—and who should know that:

> Politics having become the most lucrative business in the country, with few checks and controls, there is a compulsion for the minister or political leader to attempt to coerce civil servants to collude with him for mutual benefit . . . The service rules and procedures have been progressively adapted to facilitate this process.[4]

Again, as is the case with respect to the effects of corruption, the worst sufferers of the politicization of administration are the poor, because of their dependence on public services and government programmes for various facilities, such as subsidized food and health services. Unfortunately, the poor also face the maximum degree of indifference and harassment from government staff in securing access to what they are entitled.

The indifference of the administrative system towards the poor in providing them with their legitimate entitlements is the principal reason for the increasing disparities between urban and rural areas as well as the widening in income levels of different classes of citizens. The poor and unemployed are more dependent on the government than other sections of the people, particularly those who are employed in the organized sector and/or have access to services provided by other non-governmental sources.

In addition to control over the services provided by the government, another fertile area for reaping political benefits is the control over public-sector enterprises. Many crucial sectors of the economy are dominated by public enterprises, for example, the railways, airports, public transport, oil, steel, coal and banking and insurance. For nearly four decades after Independence, many of these sectors were also characterized by widespread controls and shortages. The powers of issuing licences and allocating distribution channels for goods and services to beneficiaries (for instance, petrol pumps) were vested with and enjoyed by political authorities in charge of different ministries.

Over the last three decades, most of the controls over the economy have been removed, and shortages of various kinds have also largely disappeared because of the abolition of import quotas, reduction in monopolies and the entry of new producers. Nevertheless, given the large role of public enterprises in the economy, the control of such enterprises still confers substantial powers to ministers-in-charge in dispensing political patronage to the suppliers and buyers of various kinds of goods and services. Large contracts for new projects also require ministerial approval after all other technical and procedural formalities have been completed. Ministries have the final say on all policy matters, for example, pricing policy or financial policy, including the issue of additional shares to the public.

The greatest impact of political control and lack of autonomy on the management of public enterprises has been on their profitability and return on capital employed. Managers of public enterprises have virtually no flexibility in respect of operational or policy issues concerning their companies, such as for the shifting of branches, choice of delivery outlets, changing of the product mix, pricing of products, redeployment of staff, raising fresh capital and corporate planning. While opportunities foregone and the inefficient use of resources often impose heavy costs on public enterprises (and on the government in those cases where direct subsidies are provided to such enterprises in the Budget), the social returns and benefits to the public are generally meagre. The state of rural infrastructure and public services (such as health and sanitation) continues to be appalling by any standard. As multiple government agencies and ministries at different levels at the Centre and the states are involved in programming and implementation, no one can be held directly responsible for diversions or other corrupt practices.

Separation of Powers

Earlier, a reference was made to the disputes that arise from time to time about the relative boundaries of powers and jurisdictions of the legislature, the executive and the judiciary. It was also noted that such disputes tend to become more frequent when the political interests of the leading parties in a coalition or their leaders is under threat. While the Constitution broadly defines the jurisdiction and responsibility of each organ of the state, in disputed cases involving the legislative or the executive branch, the final decision is left to the judgement of the judicial branch.

In a parliamentary system of government, members of legislatures as well as of the Cabinet are directly and—in some cases—indirectly elected by the people. Members of the judiciary, on the other hand, are unelected, and do not necessarily represent the 'will of the people'. The right to pass legislation belongs to the legislature, while the executive functions are supposed to be carried out under the direction of the Council of Ministers. In cases of dispute over the jurisdictional boundaries of the three branches of the state, the legislature can, with some justification, argue that it is the supreme law-making body and that the courts should not pass verdicts that have the effect of changing the legal position as approved by the representatives of the people. In defence of this position, it can be further pointed out that the courts can also be wrong. Thus, some court rulings in the past were wrong in law and had to be overturned by subsequent rulings by a higher court or a larger bench of the Supreme Court. No court, not even the Supreme Court, therefore, can be considered to be infallible.

It is true that, prima facie, some of the past constitutional judgements were indeed protective of private interests. For example, soon after Independence, in 1951, several court rulings overturned land-reform measures as being violative of the fundamental rights of landowners. The government, led by Jawaharlal Nehru, had to amend the Constitution to implement land reforms, which were considered vital for the country's economic and social progress. Similarly, in 1970, the Supreme Court had also ruled against the nationalization of banks undertaken by Mrs Indira Gandhi's government. Special legislation had to be passed by Parliament to make bank nationalization possible. A number of other instances could be cited where the judgement of the Supreme Court and other courts was not in line with popular expectations.

While all these arguments have some validity, keeping in view the recent political developments at the Centre and in the states, on balance, the long-term interests of the public and the ordinary citizen are safer when the Supreme Court continues to be the watchdog of India's democratic conventions and the final arbiter of the constitutional validity of any law or action approved by the legislature or the government of the day.

An advantage of the judiciary being the arbiter of the legality or otherwise of an executive or legislative decision is that, even if a particular verdict is wrong or socially unacceptable, it is subject to review and reversal. This is usually not the case with legislative or executive decisions unless the government of the day so decides. A citizen has no legal right to ask for a review of the decisions taken by the legislature or the executive, even if these are not in the public interest. The Right to Information Act, adopted in 2005, is an important step forward in making the executive accountable to the people directly. However, in case of any unjust or partisan decisions taken by the government, the remedy would still lie with the judiciary.

In conclusion, it is worthwhile emphasizing what the eminent jurist Nani Palkhivala, in his well-known book *We, the People*, published in 1984.[5] Commenting on the solemn declarations made by parliamentarians from time to time as being the supreme representatives of the will of the people, he had this to say:

> The myth that Parliament's will is the people's will was exploded at the election held in March 1977. Did the Parliament which (had earlier) passed the Forty-Second Amendment and which also approved of the proclamation of the emergency, represent the will of the people?. . . It is inconceivable that after having provided the most complete and comprehensive guarantees of the basic human freedoms known to any constitution of the world, the Constitution-makers still intended that any Parliament could take away those fundamental rights.

Further, on the sanctity of the Constitution, he reminded us and the future generations:

> The Constitution is not a structure of fossils like a coral reef and is not intended merely to enable politicians to play their unending game of power. It is meant to hold the country together when the raucous and fractious voices of today are lost in the silence of the centuries.

After nearly seventy years of Independence, the vision of India's founding fathers, of a rapidly growing, free and empowered country is now closer to reality than ever before. The Constitution—which, as Nani Palkhivala rightly reminded us, is not 'a structure of fossils'—must respond to the emerging realities of India's political life. Legislative norms and conventions must also ensure that politics serves the interests of the people rather than the other way around.

8

Priorities for the Future:
The Reform of Politics and Governance
in Resurgent India

Since 2011, India has been the world's third-largest economy in 'purchasing power parity' terms. Size bestows several advantages on an economy, such as a higher scale of production, with all its attendant benefits, including access to a high stock of human capital and higher productivity. That these potential advantages are not fully materializing today, despite a reasonably high rate of economic growth—and that India continues to have the largest number of persons below the poverty line in the world—points to something other than mere economics that is slowing the pace of poverty alleviation and employment generation in India. And this factor is ever-present politics.

India's history since Independence, as indeed that of other developing countries across the world, highlights the importance of politics to outcomes. In this context, an additional factor that needs to be kept in view is that the overall political situation changes from time to time, for better or for worse, which, in turn, affects the economy.

Some priorities for political reforms are highlighted below. These reforms are likely to strengthen the governance structure, alleviate poverty and make the government more accountable for its performance. The suggestions are few in number and have no party-specific agenda, either on the right or the left. Some of these political priorities have also been highlighted in the previous chapters.

Fragmentation of Parties

Under the present constitutional provisions, as a consequence of amendments carried out in 1985 and again in 2003 to prevent defections, now, there is also a 'built-in perverse incentive' for the fragmentation of political parties at the time of election. This is because the smaller a party, the greater the ability of an individual legislator to defect to another party in search of political power. Thus, for example, a member elected from a large national party has very little discretion to defect without the support of a substantial number of other members who also wish to defect. However, if the same person is a member of a small party of five or ten members, a consensus to defect among all of them, or only three or four of them, and switch from one coalition to another, is easier to achieve. The same is true of the so-called 'independent' members who are supported by some political parties during elections. In a situation where multiparty coalitions are the norm, all regional or caste leaders with a handful of constituencies naturally have a much greater incentive to form their own separate parties rather than join a large party.

In the Lok Sabha, with 543 members, a party with, say, ten or fifteen members (or even less) can join the government, enjoy ministerial berths and then delay or help in amending a cabinet decision on an important policy measure. Similarly, a party with even three or four seats can join the government and choose the portfolio that it wishes. If things don't work out, any small party or a combination of such parties can threaten to leave the government and destabilize it.

In order to reduce the present built-in incentive for the fragmentation of parties and to improve governance, it is of utmost importance that the anti-defection law be made applicable to all parties and so-called independent members who *choose* to join a coalition government in power. In other words, parties that join a coalition should not be able to defect without having to seek re-election. Such an amendment to the 'anti-defection law' will go a long way in strengthening the principle of collective responsibility of the Cabinet to the people, as enshrined in the Constitution.

Federation of States

Articles 245 to 255 of the Constitution of India deal with the distribution of powers between the Union of India and the states. The Centre has exclusive powers to make laws in respect of matters enumerated in the 'Union List' (such as defence, foreign relations and financial matters concerning the whole of India). The states have exclusive powers to make laws in respect of matters enumerated in the State List. These generally include matters where uniformity across different states in respect of legal or administrative matters is not considered necessary (such as internal law and order, agriculture, trade and commerce within a state). There is also the Concurrent List, under which both the Union and the states can make laws. These include matters where the Centre can make laws applicable to all of India, but where individual states are also entitled to pass laws of specific interest to them. The residual powers, i.e., powers to make laws on any subject that is not listed in any of the above lists rest with the Union (unlike certain other federations, such as the United States, where the residual powers are with the states). The Centre also has the powers to make laws that are applicable to two or more states, if the concerned states so request, on a matter listed in the State List.

The above scheme for distribution of powers between the Union and the states has stood the test of time and is a tribute to the foresight of the framers of India's Constitution. In a country with such great diversity in languages, religions, castes and levels of development, this scheme has proved to be a major unifying force among the different states. All states are represented in the two Houses of Parliament. In Parliament, they work together on the treasury benches or in the Opposition. Regional issues and matters of interest to particular states are open to discussion in Parliament, and are generally resolved through a consensus. There are, of course, long-standing interstate disputes (particularly with regard to water or sources of energy), which flare up from time to time. However, even these have not threatened the unity of India because of the Union's conciliatory role and the representation of most states in the Union Cabinet.

On balance, however, considering political developments at the Centre and states in the past three decades and the emergence of multiparty coalitions as a regular feature of governments in several states, it is desirable to review the present scheme of division of powers between the Union and the states. So far as the maintenance of internal and external security is concerned, there is a strong case to transfer full powers to the Centre from the states, because of the emergence of terrorist linkages across different countries as well as due to the need to maintain full social and civilian rights all over the country, as guaranteed by the Constitution. In the economic area, on the other hand, it is desirable to consider a reverse transfer, i.e., the powers and responsibility for financial development programmes as well as for implementing poverty alleviation schemes should be transferred from the Centre to the states.

In the economic area, in respect of the transfer of powers to the states, immediate action needs to be taken on two fronts. First, more financial powers and transfer of resources for implementing investment and subsidy schemes should be entrusted to the states. This is not because all states are likely to be more scrupulous or consistent in the exercise of their powers, but because greater transparency and competition among states would at least ensure that better governed states have easier access to financial resources and the opportunity to implement their programmes. Just as the Finance Commission is constitutionally empowered to decide on the division of tax resources between the Centre and the states, a similar federal commission should be statutorily set up to decide on the devolution of all other forms of central assistance. The allocation of non-tax central assistance should be related exclusively to the implementation of approved anti-poverty and development programmes in physical terms, i.e., the greater the success of a state in implementing a programme in relation to its target in quantitative terms, the higher should be the allocation of central funds to that state.

Second, all appointments in autonomous institutions, regulatory bodies, public enterprises, banks, and financial, educational and cultural institutions in the public sector should be entrusted to specialized bodies set up on the same lines as the Union Public Service Commission (UPSC). These appointment boards should follow transparent procedures for recommending appointments to the top positions. Their recommendations should be invariably accepted by the government (as is the case with UPSC recommendations for entry into the civil services and other appointments under its purview). Similar procedures, at arm's length from the government, may be adopted for top appointments in the civil services. Recent developments, and the controversies surrounding them, in many of India's top institutions—including the centres of excellence in medicine and management—highlight the need for urgent action to insulate public institutions from excessive political interference in their day-to-day work.

The Functioning of Parliament

Even after taking into account the observed decline in recent years in the role of Parliament in shaping the nation's policy priorities, the events of March 2006, as highlighted in the previous chapter, were nothing short of bizarre. The Budget and the Finance Bill were passed without sufficient notice within a couple of days. The government suddenly decided to adjourn Parliament *sine die* in the middle of the session, only to reconvene it again after a few days. During the resumed session, the controversy about members of Parliament (including high dignitaries) holding so-called 'offices of profit' reached its culmination. As per existing rules, members are not eligible to hold 'offices of profit' unless specifically exempted by Parliament. In May 2006, the government proposed—and the Parliament disposed—a new bill to exempt some specific offices at the Centre and in the states, depending on whether these offices were held by sitting members of Parliament. Thus, the same office (say, the chairmanship of the Waqf Board) was exempted in one state, because a current member was holding the office, but not in other states of the Union. The details of this controversy are not important for our purposes here; what is important is to recognize that in India's long parliamentary legislative history, the passage of this bill, some years ago, marked a new low.

If proof were needed to corroborate the above conclusion, this was amply provided by the refusal of the President of India to give assent to the bill, as passed by Parliament. For the first time after the adoption of India's Constitution, the President sent the bill back to Parliament along with his observations, for reconsideration. The government, in its wisdom, decided to place the same bill for approval by Parliament without responding to the constitutional issues raised by the President. Despite the reservations of several members, the Parliament duly approved the bill once again, as proposed by the government.

This extraordinary and unprecedented event was followed by several unsavoury controversies in July–August 2006: certain decisions taken by the Cabinet, a book by the leader of the Opposition in the Rajya Sabha and allegations of wrongdoing by a former minister of external affairs. Charges and countercharges were hurled across the floor of the two Houses from all sides. In view of noisy disruptions, Parliament had to be adjourned several times. The Speaker and the Chairman of the two Houses tried to control and direct the proceedings, but to no avail. The well-established rules of procedure for the conduct of business in the Houses of Parliament were also largely ignored. Any citizen watching the proceedings of Parliament from inside or outside (on dedicated TV channels) could not help but be dismayed by the persistent chaos and lawlessness witnessed in the highest legislative body of the largest democracy in the world during that period.

It is also significant that, in the midst of all the noise and disruption, the so-called government business was duly carried out, including the adoption of several legislative bills. Since the government bills, resolutions and statements could not be discussed because of the frequent disruptions, these were adopted by voice votes within a couple of minutes (with very few members being aware of the fact that they were actually voting!). Over time, the passage of important government bills in Parliament has become a mere formality.

It does not really matter whether Parliament meets or not; what the government wants to do is anyway done regardless, in one way or another. The responsibility of the executive to the legislature is also largely a myth and is of no particular consequence. There are, of course, occasions when debates in Parliament on important national issues are of exceptionally high quality, and the government is responsive to the concerns expressed by members in Parliament (for example, in respect of Goods and Services Tax in 2016–17).

In recent years, the responsibility of Parliament for enforcing the accountability of the multiparty executive has increased, but, unfortunately, its power to do so has diminished. In order to restore the relevance of Parliament in a parliamentary democracy, it is now imperative to take measures to make its proceedings orderly. There must be strict rules of business, which should not be violated. A possible approach for achieving this objective could be as follows:

- In theory, the Speaker and the Chairman have the powers to expel a member from the House or suspend him or her. But these powers have seldom been exercised. A convention has developed whereby the House can be adjourned several times during the day, in the event of disruption by a few members. It may be specifically provided, by legislation, that either House of Parliament cannot be adjourned more than twice in a week unless the listed business, including carried-over business from previous sessions, has been completed after full discussion as per the time allotted by the Business Advisory Committees of Parliament.

- No bill or legislative business of the government should be approved by a 'voice vote'. It should be made compulsory to adopt all bills after division and the counting of votes. This would require one or two hours of additional time to pass a bill, which is not excessive. In case the matter is considered urgent or there is a national emergency, the Speaker/Chairman should be empowered to convene a special session, where no other matter can be raised.

- A legislative provision may be made to the effect that the established rules of procedure for conduct of business of the House cannot be suspended or amended after a session of Parliament has been formally convened, except in a national emergency declared by the government with the approval of the President. In other words, the ad hoc and sudden suspension of rules of business should not normally be permitted.

- It should be made compulsory for the Budget and the Finance Bill to be passed only after consideration by the concerned standing committees of Parliament. This rule, which is already in place, should be made compulsory. If, for any reason (such as election schedules), sufficient time is not available, only then a 'vote-on-account' should be passed by Parliament.
- The Speaker/Chairman should be required mandatorily to suspend or expel the members who frequently disrupt the House. If members from any side of the House (those belonging to the ruling parties or to the parties in Opposition) disrupt the work of the House on, say, more than two occasions in a week, it should be incumbent on the Speaker/Chairman to continue with the session (by suspending or expelling defaulting members) rather than adjourn the House.

The above rules will by no means eliminate all the problems that affect the functioning of Parliament, but these will certainly help in making its sessions more purposeful.

Criminals in Politics

A related urgent political reform is to reduce the attractiveness of politics as a career of choice by persons with criminal records. There is a natural reluctance among the investigating agencies and ministries of government to speed up investigations and the prosecution of persons who are leaders of political parties and/or members of the Cabinet. According to the statistical survey of elections to the Lok Sabha in recent elections, including the 2014 elections, it has been found that nearly 20 per cent of the candidates surveyed, cutting across party lines (excluding independent candidates) had criminal antecedents. In the present Lok Sabha, which has 543 seats in all, well over 100 members had criminal cases pending against them.

The present incentive for persons who have criminal cases pending in higher courts of appeal (either the High Court or the Supreme Court) should be *effectively reversed* by giving such cases the highest priority if the concerned person is actually elected to Parliament or a State legislature. Their 'presumed' innocence should be proved within six months of election before they can take their seats in the assembly or Parliament. The fast settlement of such cases would provide a big relief to persons with criminal charges who are actually innocent and not only 'presumed' to be so. And those who are actually guilty may choose not to contest elections so that they are in a position to delay hearings through normal legal procedures!

Administrative Reforms

Another important priority is to simplify administrative procedures and reduce the number of agencies, at different levels, involved in providing clearances for undertaking any activity. For example, at least thirty different clearances involving several agencies at the Centre and the states are required for setting up even a modest-sized industrial factory. With the exception of selected areas where strict timelines can be prescribed for giving approvals (such as in the case of forest and environment clearances), it is desirable to cut through the elaborate red tape and rely primarily on 'self-certification'. The government can lay down standards and norms (for example, in respect of pollution or fire safety), and the entity concerned may be required to 'self-certify' at the highest levels of management that these have been complied with in accordance with the notified procedures. Government agencies can make random checks, and in case there are clear-cut violations, appropriate penal action can be taken. Similarly, the present complexity in regulations should be reduced drastically. Such simplification has been tried out in some areas with success (for example, with regard to foreign-exchange transactions).

A related area is transparency in the decision-making process of the government. A major step in this respect has been taken with the enactment of the Right to Information Act, 2005. The beneficial impact of this legislation in making the government accountable and citizen-friendly is already visible. A further step in this direction is to make it mandatory for all ministries and departments of the government to voluntarily make information on the decisions taken by them available to the public (excluding security-related subjects). It may be clarified that information should be released by the ministries themselves, without the need for any member of the public to ask for it. If this is done, the free media and civil-society institutions will constitute an effective instrument for enforcing accountability in the decision-making process of the government.

Case studies of international experience in the management of public services show that the objective of such programmes can be achieved better, and at a lesser cost, if a distinction is made between the ownership of these services (by the government) and the delivery of such services (by non-governmental organizations and local enterprises). In such cases, the public authorities retain the responsibility for regulating and monitoring the activities, providing subsidies where necessary and laying down distribution guidelines. In India, two noteworthy examples of public–private collaboration in the area of public services are the public call offices (PCOs) that revolutionized the availability of telephone services all over the country in the 1990s and the Sulabh Sauchalayas, which, despite some problems, are estimated to have provided sanitation facilities to more than ten million people at a very low cost.

The above suggestions for redefining the role of government in the economy are by no means exhaustive or permanent over time. The role of the government in the economy should be kept under continuous review and evolve as necessary for the benefit of the people as a whole.

Ministerial Responsibility

A minister, as the political head of a ministry, enjoys enormous executive powers. Part of the rationale for entrusting politically appointed ministers, of whom several have very little previous administrative experience, is that the ministry is supposed to be accountable to the Cabinet and to Parliament through them.

While the above system is sound in principle, in practice there has been a substantial erosion in the ability of Parliament/legislatures to hold ministers responsible, either collectively or individually, for the decisions taken by them on behalf of their ministries. In addition to the principle of collective responsibility (which shields ministers from taking individual responsibility), another reason why ministers are not held accountable is that most subjects of direct interest to the public in the economic area are in the Concurrent or State Lists of business. The Central ministers are free to make pronouncements, approve policy guidelines and set all-India targets, but the actual implementation of many programmes is in the hands of individual states. A familiar excuse given by Central ministers for their failure in meeting the targets announced by them is that the states are responsible, not the Centre. The states, on the other hand, blame the Centre for the inadequate allocation of funds, inappropriate guidelines or approval delays by one or more ministries at the Centre. The present situation, where the Central ministers are quick to announce policies and targets for removing poverty or illiteracy, but where they take no responsibility for achieving these targets, is clearly untenable.

An important political priority for the future is to ensure that whatever annual targets are announced by a ministry (in consultation with other concerned ministries) are carefully reviewed for their feasibility in implementation. Once an annual target is announced by a ministry, it should have the full authority to implement it, and it should be the ministry itself that is held accountable for the actual performance. If there is a change of ministers during the course of the year, then the new minister must once again affirm or change the target with the approval of Parliament.

Depoliticization of Bureaucracy

The basic issue that needs to be tackled for improving the morale of the civil service is really that of the 'separation of powers' within the executive—between ministers and civil servants—insofar as postings, transfers, promotions, and other similar administrative matters are concerned. The separation of powers among the three branches of the government—the executive, the legislature and the judiciary—is already enshrined in the Constitution. Although there has been considerable encroachment of the executive powers into the legislative—and even judicial—areas (as well as the other way around), it can still be said that these three separate branches enjoy a certain measure of autonomy and independence. Within the executive branch, as it happens, the civil service has become, over time, completely dependent on the pleasure of the ministers with regard to even the most mundane and routine administrative matters. It is essential to revert to a rule-based system of administration, which circumscribes the powers of politicians and confers greater authority on the civil service itself for self-regulation.

The greater empowerment of the civil service must, of course, go hand in hand with the greater accountability of civil servants for their performance and ethical conduct. Part of the reason for the insensitivity of civil servants to the concerns of the public is the unlimited protection provided to 'public servants' under the Constitution and various judicial pronouncements. In view of the time-consuming process of inquiries and judicial delays, the possibility of any penal action for even the most blatant actions of civil servants is considered remote. They may be apprehended and sent to judicial custody for a few days. Thereafter, more often than not, they are released on bail, and enjoy complete freedom of action, including the right to contest elections after their retirement from service.

Except for the security, police and defence services, the constitutional protection provided to civil servants needs to be withdrawn. They should be covered under the country's normal rules and laws that are applicable to other citizens, employees and workers. Two statutory provisions, in particular, namely Article 311 of the Constitution and the Official Secrets Act, 1923, require urgent reconsideration. Article 311 provides comprehensive constitutional protection, which has been widely misused, for a person holding 'a civil post from being reduced in rank, removed or dismissed from service'. The Official Secrets Act, 1923, provides protection to civil servants and ministers from being held accountable for any action that can be labelled secret by them. The Right to Information Act, 2005, has substantially reduced the power of civil servants to deny information to the public. There is no reason why the 1923 Act should still remain valid.

It may be clarified that the withdrawal of constitutional and special statutory protection provided to civil servants will not, in any way, affect their service conditions, pay and other benefits. These will continue to be determined as per the present rules and procedures.

Rationalization of Subsidies

An important political priority for the future is to further rationalize the system of delivery of public services to the people, particularly subsidies for various essential items such as food, health and education for persons below the poverty line. An important recent initiative in this respect is the scheme for Direct Benefits Transfers (DBT) in respect of food subsidies across the country. The total number of Centrally Sponsored Schemes (CSS), which are spread over several sectors and departments with different designs and funding patterns, have also been reduced in 2013–14 from 142 to sixty-six. However, despite the reduction in the number of schemes, the outcomes in terms of actual benefits to the poor have been relatively small.

At present, each subsidy scheme has its own delivery and administrative apparatus, with consequent costs. Further action over the next couple of years to merge, rationalize and converge schemes to a much lower number should now be initiated based on three basic principles:

i. Convert all schemes to cash transfers through public-sector agencies as well as private service providers;
ii. Merge schemes with significant overlaps, with largely common beneficiaries and objectives; and
iii. Ensure the decentralization of delivery mechanism to states who can also be empowered to design specific schemes in ways that meet the objectives laid down by the Centre, depending on the prevailing local circumstances.

These measures would certainly help significantly in reducing costs and increasing actual benefits to the people.

To conclude, it may be mentioned that the above political priorities for reforms are few in number. There is, of course, a lot more that can be done to tackle the challenges of the future. It may be recalled that in the earlier years after Independence, there was considerable scepticism about India's ability to even survive as a democracy in the long run. It was the vision of Jawaharlal Nehru and other political leaders, and the personal examples set by them, which made it possible. Similarly, in the 1980s, after years of slow growth and periodic crises, the then prime ministers were able to initiate a process of economic reforms that gave India some stability and revival of growth. Again, in the early 1990s, during one of the worst economic crises, when prospects for India were regarded as hopeless, the government was able to launch a programme of action that proved to be highly successful.

If the above suggestions are implemented over the next couple of years by the current government in power, there is no doubt that India will be in a position to realize its full potential as one of the fastest-growing emerging global powers and to ensure that the benefits of growth reach all the people, particularly the disadvantaged sections of our society.

Notes

Chapter 1: Development Strategy and Performance

1. Ragnar Nurkse, 'Pattern of Trade and Development', Wicksell Lectures, reprinted in S. Haberler and R.M. Stern, *Equilibrium and Growth in the World Economy*, Cambridge: Mass., 1961.
2. Simon Kuznets, 'Towards a Theory of Economic Growth' in Levachman R., ed., *National Policy for Economic Welfare at Home and Abroad* (New York: Doubleday & Co., 1955).
3. Paul N. Rosentein-Rodan (1943), 'Problems of Industrialization in Eastern and South-Eastern Europe', *Economic Journal*, vol. 53, pp. 202–11.
4. Tibor Scitovsky (1954), 'Two Concepts of External Economies', *Journal of Political Economy*, vol. 62.
5. Raúl Prebisch (1950), *The Economic Development of Latin America*, United Nations.
6. W.A. Lewis (1954), 'Economic Development with Unlimited Supplies of Labor', reprinted in A.N. Agarwala and S.P. Singh, (eds.), *The Economics of Underdevelopment* (London: Oxford University Press, 1954).
7. Paul Kennedy, *The Rise and Fall of the Great Powers* (New York: Vintage Books, 1989).

Chapter 2: Controls, Regulations and the State

1. *Economic Survey 1994–1995*, Ministry of Finance, Government of India, 1995; available online at http://indiabudget.nic.in/es1994-95/esmain.htm.
2. Sukhamoy Chakravarty, *Development Planning: The Indian Experience* (Oxford: Clarendon Press, 1987).
3. Paul Kennedy, *Preparing for the Twenty-first Century* (New York: Vintage Books, 1994).
4. Atul Kohli, *Democracy and Discontent: India's Growing Crisis of Governability* (Cambridge: Cambridge University Press, 1991).

Chapter 3: After the Crisis: Need for a New Strategy

1. M. Scott, *A New View of Economic Growth* (Oxford: Clarendon Press, 1989). Also 'Policy Implications of a New View of Economic Growth', *Economic Journal*, vol. 102, No. 412, May 1992.
2. Martin Ricketts, *Financial Times,* 29 June 1992.
3. V.M. Dandekar, 'Forty Years after Independence', in Bimal Jalan (ed.), *The Indian Economy* (London: Penguin, 1992).

Chapter 4: Finance and Development: A Shifting Paradigm

1. Jagdish Bhagwati, 'Wheel of Fortune', *New Republic,* 5 October 1987, reproduced in *A Stream of Windows: Unsettling Reflections on Trade, Immigration and Democracy* (Cambridge: MIT Press, 1998).
2. P.S. Jha, 'South East Asia and the Future of the Global Economy', *World Affairs*, New Delhi, July–September, 1999.
3. Y.V. Reddy, 'Financial Sector Reform: Review and Prospects', reprinted in *Reserve Bank of India Bulletin,* January 1999. For a recent review of financial-sector issues by experts, see

J.A. Hanson and S. Kathuria, *India: A Financial sector for the Twenty-first Century* (New Delhi: Oxford University Press, 1999).

Chapter 5: India's Economy in the Twenty-first Century: A New Beginning or a False Dawn?

1. Mervyn King, 'A Tale of Two Cities' (speech, Cardiff Business School, Cardiff University, 18 June 2001).
2. Paul Krugman, *The Return of Depression Economics* (London: Penguin Books, 1999).
3. W.A. Lewis, 'Economic Development with Unlimited Supplies of Labour', *Manchester School* 22, no. 2 (May 1954).
4. Hanson A.H., 'The Crisis of Indian Planning', *Political Quarterly* (October–December 1963), reprinted in Hanson A.H. *Planning and Politicians* (London: Routledge and Kegan Paul, 1969).
5. Kirit Parikh, 'Economy' in *India Briefing: Transformative Fifty Years* (New York: M.E. Sharpe, 1999).
6. J.A. Rosenzweig, *Winning the Global Game* (New York: The Free Press, 1998).

Chapter 6: Politics and Governance

1. Gunnar Myrdal, *Economic Theory and Underdeveloped Regions* (London: Methuen & Co., 1957).
2. I.M.D. Little, '*Ethics, Economics and Politics: Principles of Public Policy*' (New Delhi: Oxford University Press, 2003).
3. Pratap Bhanu Mehta, *The Burden of Democracy* (New Delhi: Penguin, 2003).
4. J.A. Rosenzweig, *Winning the Global Game* (New York: The Free Press, 1998).
5. Kirit Parikh, 'Economy' in *India Briefing: Transformative Fifty Years* (New York: M.E. Sharp, 1999).

Chapter 7: Separation of Powers: The Myth and the Reality

1   Report of the National Commission to Review the Working of the Constitution, 2002, Government of India, New Delhi, p. 105.
2   Ibid., p.124.
3   Rajiv Gandhi, cited in *India Today*, 30 November 1989.
4   T.S.R. Subramanian, 'All the Netaji's Men', *Indian Express*, 25 September 2004.
5   N.A. Palkhivala, *We, the People* (Mumbai: Strand Book Store, 1984).

Index

accountability, 62, 66, 67, 120; of administrative organs of the state, 72; of civil servants, 114–15, 160; of the Council of Ministers, 102, 115, 135–36, 138; of the executive to the Parliament, 153; financial, 88; of the government in decision-making process, 157; of the government to the judiciary, 105–6; of the government to Parliament, 104; non-accountability, 115

accounting practices, 60

administration, 6, 20, 24–25, 98, 110, 112; personnel, 87; politicization, 138–42

administrative: changes, xiii; complexity, 29, 121; control, 16; costs/

expenditure, xiv, 111; decisions, 134–35; functions, 35, 159–60, 161; hurdles, 35; implications of policies, 99; inefficiencies and bottlenecks, 108, 111, 121; processes, 111; realities, 110; reforms, 122, 156–58; requirements, 6; resources and capability, constraints, 16, 21; rules, 93; salaries and pensions, 114; structure, 6–7, 113, 118; system and economic development, xiii, xiv, 113, 116–17, 120, 122, 138, 141, advertising, 87

agriculture, 7, 27, 29, 112, 148; credit and rural banking, 69; and

169

capital adequacy ratio, 64, 65
capital flows, 34, 58–59
capital formation, 16, 35; in manufacturing, growth, 42
capital goods, 8; taxation of imports, 49
capital investments, 78
capital market, 4, 20, 26, 54, 63, 68, 89
capital movements, 58, 107
capital-output ratio, 11, 42, 83
capital replacement, 49
capital stock, changes, 41
cash reserve ratio, 61–62, 63
caste, 100, 104, 149; and religion, 103
centrally sponsored schemes (CSS), 161
China, 33, 71; agricultural income, 10; economic growth, 97–98; human development index, 11–12; and India war (1962), 15
civil services, civil servants, 105, 115, 151; accountability, 120, 160–61; corruption, 119, 139–40; depoliticization, 159; empowerment, 160; and political leadership, division of roles, 116, 147, 160; politicization, 133, 138; powers and role in

decision-making process, 115; and private sector, 114; problems, 114
coalition governments/politics, 22, 97, 101–2, 104, 147–49; compulsions of, xii, 108, 126, 128–29, 134, 136, 137, 143
collective responsibility, notion of, 115, 133–38
colonial state and income stagnation, 79
Committee on Banking Sector Reforms (Narasimham Committee II, 1997), 62–63, 67
communication, 12, 85; decline in costs, 33, 87; policy, 37; services, 87; technology, 86
comparative advantage, 32–34, 71, 78, 107
competition, 7, 21, 45, 62, 64, 150
Congress, xii, 96, 113
Constituent Assembly, 125
Constitution of India, 100, 102–5, 119, 148–50, 152, 160–61; 42nd Amendment, 145; doctrine of 'basic structure, 105, 133; doctrine of separation of powers, 116, 125–45, 159

Emerging India: Economics, Politics and Reforms

As India marks the twenty-year milestone of economic liberalization, some concerns about the country's future prospects as an emerging power are beginning to be voiced; often, these stem from the past history of sharp swings in India's fortunes. Bimal Jalan, one of the country's well-known economists and former Governor of the Reserve Bank of India, has closely followed the path of India's economic policies across its changing trajectories, from before the time the economy was liberalized to the very present The pieces that appear here were all written during the last twenty years, with the exception of three prescient notes from the mid-1970s highlighting the need for economic reforms to foster growth. The principal thought behind these essays is that, in the past twenty years, India's capacity to grow faster than ever before has increased substantially because of its comparative advantage in relation to other countries. However, Jalan points out that for India to seize the opportunities that lie ahead, it is essential to bring about further reforms in the running of India's politics and administration in order to ensure inclusive and incremental economic growth.

Non-Fiction/PB

India's Politics: A View from the Backbench

An insider's account of how politics is practised in India, and to what effect

In India's Politics: A View from the Backbench, Bimal Jalan, ex-Governor of the Reserve Bank of India and best-selling author of *The Future of India*, turns his gaze to the complex mechanics of the political system in the country. As a member of Parliament, Bimal Jalan has watched the workings of India's politics closely. While there is much to be proud of in India's achievements as a vibrant democracy, there are some areas of concern, which require attention. In particular, Jalan finds that the emergence of multiparty coalitions as a regular form of government—and their relatively short life expectancy at birth—has brought about a sea change in political dynamics. The search for power and the compulsions of coalition politics are increasingly the primary drivers of political behaviour in India today. This development, combined with the need to cope with global terrorism, lawlessness and economic disparities during a period of high growth, calls for some urgent reforms in the working of India's vital political institutions. Jalan puts forward a ten-point programme to make India's parliamentary democracy more stable, transparent and accountable. According to him, constant vigilance is indeed the price of liberty and if some of the emerging trends are not reversed, India's democracy 'by the people' could become more and more oligarchic—'of the few and for the few'. *India's Politics* is one of the most important studies of India's political system to have been written. This paperback edition features a new Preface by the author on emerging political trends.

Non-Fiction/PB

The Future of India: Politics, Economics and Governance

As recently as a decade ago, the prospect of India becoming a developed country any time soon seemed a distant possibility. Since then, however, there has been a sea change in our own and the world's perception about our future. What explains this rising tide of optimism? And how far is it justified? In the future of India, Bimal Jalan, former Governor of the Reserve Bank of India, takes up the formidable challenge of examining the nuts and bolts of this proposition. In his thought-provoking, clear-sighted analysis, he argues that it is the interface between politics, economics and governance, and their combined effect on the functioning of our democracy, which will largely determine India's future. An understanding of this interface will help explain the swings in India's political and economic fortunes over the past decades, and why the promise has been belied. In the light of experience, argues Jalan, there is no certainty that the present euphoria will last unless there is the political will to seize the new opportunities that are available. He proceeds to suggest steps that can be taken to smoothen our path to progress: ways to strengthen Parliament and the judiciary; a series of political reforms that would, among other things, see greater accountability among ministers; and effective ways to curb corruption and enhance fiscal viability. In all these there is an emphasis on the pragmatic, born of Jalan's experience as an administrator, economist and member of Parliament. Contemporary and topical, *The Future of India: Politics, Economics and Governance*, perhaps more than any other book on the subject, shows just how a future close enough to be seen need not forever remain elusive to the grasp.

Non-Fiction/PB

ALSO BY THE SAME AUTHOR

India's Economic Policy: Preparing for the Twenty-first Century

A lucid and brilliantly argued book on India's recent economic reforms. Nearly fifty years after Independence, India remains a very poor country. It ranks near the bottom in terms of per capita income, and is similarly placed in the Human Development Index that measures social well-being. Economic growth in India has been less than half that of China or even other countries in Asia. And governments, at the Centre as well as in the states, are close to insolvency. The reason for our spectacular underachievement lies in the continuation of policies which had a certain validity as a response to the colonial experience, but which have long outlived their usefulness. The global economic scene has changed dramatically since they were formulated, and we must respond to the new realities. Bimal Jalan, the well-known economist and former Governor of the RBI, in this lucid and well-argued book, makes a case for governments doing what they alone can best do, and less of what they cannot do effectively.

Business/PB

The Indian Economy: Problems and Prospects

The Indian Economy: Problems and Prospects, first published in 1992, looks at the country's economy and the resolved fiscal crisis from a historical perspective. Edited and updated with a new Introduction by Bimal Jalan, the book retains the thirteen essays written by eminent economic thinkers in 1991 and 1992 in their original form as they provide a comprehensive overview of India's economic development since Independence and answer questions on key economic issues that are as relevant today as they were at that time. Bipan Chandra conducts a historical survey of fiscal developments during the colonial period, the late V.M. Dandekar evaluates India's economic performance from 1950 to 1990, and Rakesh Mohan traces the history of industrial controls from the pre-Independence era. Also included are essays by C.H. Hanumantha Rao, C. Rangarajan and Narendra Jadhav, Raja Chelliah, Sudipto Mundle and M. Govinda Rao, Jyoti and Kirit Parikh, Pravin Visaria, T.S. Papola, Pranab Bardhan and Kaushik Basu. In his revised Introduction, Bimal Jalan assesses the country's economic progress since 1991, examines crucial events and their relative significance. Exploring diverse aspects of the Indian economy as well as the political, institutional and legal implications of economic reforms, these insightful and revelatory essays will be of enormous interest to experts and the general reader alike.

Business/PB